JESUS AND
THE RACING RAT

GEOFF SHATTOCK

PRAISE FOR:
JESUS AND THE RACING RAT

"When you see these principles, they seem obvious; it's just that it takes someone like Geoff Shattock to help you see them."
Steve Chalke MBE
Founder, Oasis Trust

"Finally some good news for the rat race. For those of us who live our lives at a ridiculous pace, this book is literally a godsend. It is a breath of fresh air for exhausted workers."
Professor Cary Cooper
Professor of Organizational Psychology and Health,
Lancaster University

"When you read Jesus and the Racing Rat, you will be able to see for yourself what I have come to understand, admire, and love, namely that Geoff is truly committed to helping people live out the principles of working well. It is not just an intellectual exercise. Geoff seeks to transform lives so we can truly be good news to the people that have been placed in our sphere of influence."
William Pezzutti
Vice President of Client Services and Director of Risk Management,
Harden & Associates

"In Jesus and the Racing Rat, you will see that Geoff Shattock is able to discern characteristics in others that may not be obvious even to themselves. With wise application of spiritual principles, he gives encouragement and advice that is invaluable to your ongoing lifestyle."
Bruce Streather
Founder and Senior Partner, Streather's Solicitors LLP

"Geoff's writings are an extension of Geoff the man; they are always characterized by emotional empathy, spiritual insight, and razor-sharp wit. Geoff is a master at engaging and challenging his audience."
Kim Taplin
Chaplain, Clifton College

"Geoff Shattock's rich background in stress research and stress management at the workplace, combined with his intense faith, enable him to provide profound insights into how Jesus of Nazareth dealt with His own workplace situations. Jesus and the Racing Rat translates a perfect strategy into very applicable guidelines on how to prevent or reverse the stressful fragmentation of life into competing work, family, and worship splinters."

Dr. Clive H. Wilder-Smith, MD, AGAF, FRCP (Edinburgh, Scotland)
Professor of Medicine, Specialist Gastroenterologist, and Director of Brain-Gut Research Group

"A wise friend once told me we should pay special attention to what a person says toward the end of his or her life. Embedded in their words will be unusual profundity. In Jesus and the Racing Rat, Geoff Shattock unpacks the last words of Jesus of Nazareth in a remarkable way, uniquely applying them to the workplace. The content and writing style is captivating and very helpful. You will be deeply enriched by his insights."

John D. Beckett
Chairman of The Beckett Companies and Author of *Loving Monday* and *Mastering Monday*

"It isn't often that I come across a resource that equals this. Timely and much needed, it is written by an authentic pioneer and practitioner. Geoff fully captures the essence of what it means to be real in the world of work. It's fresh, sound, and provides a way of living out the life we are intended to live during the working week."

Dr. Ron Rowe
Executive Director, Jacksonville Baptist Association

"Many people spend half their waking life in 'the rat race.' Don't read this book if you don't want to be challenged, provoked, or made to think about your working life."

Derek Beal, Chief Financial Officer, Reed Global

"Geoff Shattock is a generous, multi-talented man. When you read this book, remember that he is also a songwriter, poet, guitarist, and performer. When you hear him speak, remember that he is also a writer. When you see him on video or the internet, try to get into his lively presence at some time in the future. You will reap a different benefit, you will experience another angle on his spiritually based teaching... and he will probably make you laugh too...."

Jeremy Clare

Founder, Whatever Next Consultancy

Author, *Whatever Next?*

"Geoff Shattock invites you to go on a journey of profound discovery, to explore new ways of thinking, and acquire practical toolkits for your working life. You will not be disappointed."

John Wyatt, FRCP, FRCPCH

Professor of Ethics & Perinatology University College, London

Author, *Matters of Life and Death*

"Geoff has a one-off ability to offer practical training for real people who need to cope with the challenges of 21st-century workplaces. The fact that he does it by applying a unique understanding of how a first-century carpenter and preacher worked marks Geoff's own work as inspired and inspirational."

Mark Sheard

Founder and Marketing Director, What Next Consultancy

"How do you handle stress? Jesus and the Racing Rat provides insights far beyond the typical self-help book. Combining deep spiritual truths with the practical experience of a trained professional adds up to very creative and life-changing applications. Every Christian should read this book."

Os Hillman, president, Marketplace Leaders, author *The 9 to 5 Window* and *Today God is First*

JESUS AND
THE RACING RAT

**HOW A MAN WHO CHANGED THE WORLD
CAN CHANGE THE WAY YOU WORK**

GEOFF SHATTOCK

WORKTALK
Jacksonville Florida, U.S.A.
London, England

www.racingrat.gs

ISBN: 978-0-9553560-7-0

First edition published in 2009 by:
Worktalk
PO BOX 351257,
Jacksonville, Florida 32235-1257
www.worktalk.gs
racingrat@worktalk.gs

A catalogue record of this book is available from the British Library.
US Library of Congress Control Number (LCCN): 2009935236.

Edited by David T. Brown
Project managed by Justine Koukoulis
Art direction by Martin Lambie-Nairn
Cover and interior design by Paul Franklin
Photography by Jonathan Tickner
Type-setting by Chris Gander

Printed in the United States of America

DEDICATION

For the racers I hold in my memories
To the racers I'll meet in my dreams
And the racer who opened my eyes to see
That nothing is quite what it seems

– Geoff Shattock, 2009

CONTENTS:
THE RACE PLAN

Acknowledgments: 12
My Running Mates

Author's Note: 14
Ten Reasons Why You Should Read This Book –
And Five Why You Shouldn't

Warm Up: 16
Ready? Set. Race!

Lap One: 30
Stress Reduction – The Forgiving Soul

Lap Two: 62
The Power of Hope – Whispers of Paradise

Lap Three: 82
A Balanced Life – The Meaning of Moments

Lap Four: 116
Struggle and Integrity – The God-Forsaken Path

Lap Five: 136
Being Yourself – The Obvious Heart

Lap Six: 158
Getting Things Done – The Real Deal

Lap Seven: 184
Spiritual Nourishment – The Grass by the Water

Cool Down: 208
Metaskills – Perfecting the Whole

Stretches: 216
Quotes, Notes, and Poems – The Last Surprise

About the Author: 230
The Race so Far

Related Resources   234

Space For Your Race: 238
Pages For Your Notes

ACKNOWLEDGEMENTS: MY RUNNING MATES

No book is written by the author alone, and I want to thank, pay tribute to, and acknowledge a selection of fellow runners who have helped me to bring this journey to life. They are family, friends, colleagues, and associates.

Unique thanks to my wife, Maria, who has shared my race through pleasure, pain, joy, and sorrow. To my daughter, Suzy, who has, just by being herself, provided a million moments of insight.

To my Chairman, Simon Constantine, for doing and being the real deal and thus making things materialize. To the Worktalk Board for employing the unemployable so the improbable could become possible. To my editor, Dave Brown, for a light touch and a steady hand. To Martin Lambie-Nairn, Paul Franklin, and Chris Gander for making it look as it should. To Bill and Rosie Pezzutti for opening their hearts, and Tom and Jenny Abbott for opening their homes. To all the following, who I hope know what they mean to me.

Jane Campion, Peter Church, Ray Crudgington, Stanley Dakin, Pete Hammond, David and Peggy Heron, Joy Madeiros, Tim Maynard, Eliza Nearn, John Pagden, Maureen Rose, Ron Rowe, Godfrey Rust, Cynthia Sayward, Bruce and Geraldine Streather, Bill Stroup, Nick Tanna, Max Turner, Clive Wilder-Smith, and John Wyatt.

Lastly, special thanks to my executive assistant, Justine Koukoulis, who typed the manuscript, managed the project, and made the tea. But more than that, she saw between the lines, managed the author, and made the difference.

"Friends know the song in your heart and sing it back to you when you forget the words." – Attributed to Eleanor Roosevelt

AUTHOR'S NOTE: TEN REASONS WHY YOU SHOULD READ THIS BOOK –

AND FIVE WHY YOU SHOULDN'T

YOU SHOULD READ THIS BOOK IF...

1. You would like to reduce unnecessary stress in your work and life.
2. You would like to create a climate of encouragement at your work.
3. You want to live a balanced life without being a bore.
4. You want to work with integrity, being true to your values and beliefs.
5. You want to do your job well without becoming an obsessive perfectionist.
6. You'd like to be yourself at work.
7. You'd like to find daily meaning while earning daily bread.
8. You are a follower of Jesus of Nazareth and would like to see how he tackled the exact same issues that you face at work.
9. You are not a follower of Jesus of Nazareth but would still like to see how he tackled the exact same issues that you face at work.
10. You'd like to see how a man who changed the world can change the way you work.

YOU SHOULD NOT READ THIS BOOK IF...

1. You don't like thinking deeply.
2. You believe that work is all about money, power, and status.
3. You are stress-free, always encouraging, perfectly balanced, completely integrated, always true to yourself, regularly get the job done, and never lose sight of the deeper meaning of things (If this is you, you should be writing your own book, not reading mine!)
4. You are allergic to any notion of "spirituality" or "Christian."
5. You're too busy to go on a voyage of discovery.

On second thought, you just might like to read this book anyway.

WARM UP:
READY? SET. RACE!

A noise brings you out of sleep. Or perhaps you were already awake and waiting. Depending on your style, you reluctantly or enthusiastically lurch or leap out of bed to join billions of others on the journey from being awake to being at work. Congratulations, you have become a member of the rat race.

Once the race is on, you realize your alarm was a starting gun. There is now no time to snooze and you will have to race – slowly, quickly – at a sprint or at a crawl, for at least the next eight hours.

The early laps find some racers rising to get their children ready, organizing the corporate chaos which is the family breakfast. There are many variants of this phase of the race as screaming toddlers and moribund teenagers join the discordant dawn chorus. For some, this time is full of thrills. For the not-so-early birds, this is the time of torture.

For a while, the rat race and the school run overlap but sooner or later all the runners find their places and the main part of the race unfolds. These are the hours of achievement, anguish, tedium, or fascination, which make up that most universal of experiences – the work day.

The rat race statistics are staggering. Work is the single largest consumer of our waking hours. From cradle to grave, we configure our lives around the expenditure of energy in order to achieve our goals of success, status, significance, and at its most basic, survival.

For humankind, it has been like this not just since this morning but since the dawn of civilization. We have worked to craft our culture and shape our worlds to conform to our agendas and itineraries. We have allied and divided, incorporated and associated, sole traded and globalized, merged and acquired, collaborated and competed to explore, explain, and exploit. The rat race is a marathon, a relay, a dash, and a steeplechase all at once. But race we must and race we will, and you can't pull out if you want to win. Even if you retire, you will still depend on the results of other rats to provide the conditions for you to continue running at your leisurely grey-haired pace.

This race is the journey where dreams are realized or lost and characters are built or destroyed. It is a place of love and hate, peace and war, high stakes and cheap shots, delight and drudgery. It is the race of all races and all members of the human race are caught up in its drama.

ENTER THE ENEMY

But there is a high casualty rate in this race. The pace and power needed to succeed inevitably take their toll. Even as you read my description and customize it to your experience, you will sense the rising enemy within. Perhaps we should call it a pandemic or a disease. Maybe it is best described as a disability or fault line. After all these years of racing, most people know its name. And even if they are not sure what it means they use it to cover the catalogue of pain which accompanies their own racer's experience.

You will have seen its effects either on your running style or that of others. It will have, at least occasionally, slowed you down or lost you a few places in the order of things. You will have seen some fall, · paralyzed or mesmerized, and others just exhausted by its impact.

We have studied it, analyzed it, experimented, and dissected it, and we have all agreed on its name – stress.

And there you have it. It is the blight of the racing rat, the incapacitating condition which creeps up on you, taps you on the shoulder, and hurts your back, neck, or head. It keeps you from sleeping or waking up. It gives you rashes, itches, viruses, and anxieties. It makes you cry or scream. It causes you to lose your temper or your mind. It makes your heart race, your mouth dry, and your hair stand on end.

It can stunt your growth, weaken your muscles, mess with your hormones, and make you vulnerable to major killers. From the top of your skull to the tip of your feet, stress will weave its sinister way into your own personal race and mess you up.

Now, some racers are a lot less prone to its effects than others. But because we don't race alone, if your fellow racers are struggling and you need them to perform, your race will be damaged whether you like it or not.

The stress pandemic can cause you to question your style and approach. And on a deeper level, it invites you to wonder what the point of the race is at all. Why race when the price is so high? Why race when you seem to spend more time with rats you don't really like when your loved rats are racing somewhere else? Why race so hard? Why race to win? Why am I in a part of the race which bores me to tears? Why is my race run for the benefit of others while I'm shriveling up inside and wasting my skills?

But still you race, and still you stress. Coaches shout help or self-help instructions as they race past you making a fortune out of their advice. Schools of management invite you take a pit stop and spend some time on a treadmill to improve your racing muscles But still you race and still you stress because that is how it has always been. And you have to eat; you have to earn; and you have to employ – yourself, others, or your skills.

Such is the life of the racing rat.

ENTER THE FRIEND

Sometime long after the dawn of civilization and long before your last breakfast, a different kind of racer stepped out of the blue and onto the track. The statistics of his race are nothing short of staggering. Like you, he had one shot at the run. He spent 30 years acquiring skills and 36 months doing public work. He reached the finish line via 360 excruciating minutes of dying, during which he spoke seven sentences of last words.

And yet, two thousand years after he crossed his finish line, about one-third of the entire global population run with his name on their lips, his symbol around their necks, and his words in their minds. One way or another, they claim to be his followers.

So here's a reasonable question: How did he manage, in such a short space of time (less than half of what most of us get), to run in such a way as to change the world permanently? Surely someone whose work has so profoundly inspired and influenced billions of other racers must have something to show us about how to run this rat race.

So here we come to the central question behind this book: How can a man who changed the world change the way you work?

Now I'm assuming you want to run your race well. As a realist, you know that some racing days will be painful and apparently fruitless. But as an idealist (and why not be an idealist?), you carry dreams of fulfilling your potential and finding daily meaning while earning your daily bread. Given that you spend so much of your time, energy, and resources on your race, you don't want to fall at every hurdle or turn your ankle at every bend.

But it is a race and you don't have limitless time. You can't read every book or hear every story. You can't try every diet or exercise routine.

So my suggestion is to run next to the best and grab all the lessons you can. That is what this book is about.

I'm inviting you to explore whether a carpenter from Nazareth who ran his race all those years before you and achieved so much could have something to offer you as a coach while you run yours? Could it be that the story of what was achieved during a race run in ancient times could teach us how to achieve in the modern world? From my racing experience so far, I am going to suggest to you that it can. I am confident that there are resources from yesterday's work for today's workers. There is a case for combining old wisdom and new challenges, timeless lessons, and time-poor people. In short, it's time to take a long, hard look at Jesus and the racing rat.

As we look, we will see him cope with his stress and we will watch him react to enormous pressure. We will hear how he dispensed hope, captured powerful moments, and juggled competing priorities. We will eavesdrop on his struggle with discouragement and isolation and stand by him as he stands alone with integrity. We will see how he managed to be real and true to himself with no split between public persona and private behavior. We will follow him as he got things done properly and achieved what he set out to do. We will taste the same spirituality that nourished his soul as he did the work he was born to do. As we do, we will look through windows into his soul and go behind the scenes in this most historic of dramas to discover seven secrets from the racer who changed the world. And this will change the way we race. To help you see all these things, I will need to run beside you and tell you something of my own race.

A MIDSUMMER NIGHT'S DREAM

In January 1997, well into my own race, I set off on a journey to see if the faith I had held since I was a child could be integrated into the work that I do as an adult. More importantly, I wanted to discover if it could be connected with the work *you* do as an adult. Let me explain.

There is a delicious irony here. Despite being a qualified physiologist, my chosen career path was to ordination and work within the Christian church. My faith had become my work and vice versa.

Yet, as the years passed, it became clear to me that the mere possession of a faith did not necessarily transfer into the realities of my working day. Now if it was hard enough for me who was earning a living from my faith to integrate it into my work, how much harder would it be for those whose work was not even vaguely related to faith? How could someone in a trade, profession, or business connect the faith in their souls with the work in their weeks? Harder still, how could someone with no explicit faith at all even consider the spiritual dimension to be worth exploring in their working lives?

So for seven years I labored at this experiment. I earned a master's degree in stress management. I wrote a book on faith and friendship in the workplace. I struggled for four years to become a consultant at a major training provider, offering my courses on anger management and balancing home and work. I worked with others to design retreats to help pressurized individuals find a better future by exploring their present condition. I sat with workers in all kinds of employment to listen to their issues. And I kept re-branding my skills and materials to apply them to real concerns and challenges while continually exploring my own faith to figure out its relevance to the marketplace.

Then a strange thing happened to me. One midsummer night, I went to bed thinking about some aspect of my work, as I often do. During the night I had a dream. It was concerning the design of a learning program. I had been delivering training courses for more than 20 years and I had never had the content of one come to me in a dream. I always have had great trouble remembering my dreams, but this night was different. I woke up the next day and wrote down what I had dreamed. It had been one of those nights where the lines between thoughts and dreams, and sleep and wakefulness had been blurred but the result remained crystal clear in my mind.

That night I had a spiritual experience. I shouldn't be surprised because I believe in spiritual experiences. I believe God speaks in dreams and I believe in Divine intervention. To add irony to irony, I had been longing to discover a more powerful connection between spirituality and work. Yet when it happened I was taken aback. It was as if God whispered in the night, "Look at it this way." As my perspective suddenly changed, I realized my work had been clustering around seven areas for the last seven years. I realized that there was a more powerful way of presenting the material and that this was the breakthrough I had been hoping and incidentally, praying for.

I'm well aware that Freudians will have an explanation for my midsummer night's dream, and that does not worry me. The more important issue for me is whether the results of dreams can change people's work and lives. I know they have changed mine. For seven years I had been busting a gut to solve a problem. Seven years of frenetic activity were almost certainly necessary for me to know what to do with the dream and how to develop the ideas. But after chasing my tail for what seemed like an eternity, this was a night to remember. This was a night to change lanes and run more effectively. This was the night when Jesus met me, another racing rat.

You don't have to turn over a new leaf to explore the dream. You don't even have to have a faith. You just have to turn the page and make up your own mind. To help you start to explore the dream and make up your own mind, let me tell you one short story.

A BARBEQUE ON MOUNT CARMEL

Israel – a few years ago. My wife and I were visiting long-standing friends who we had met originally in London. The husband was in the U.S. diplomatic corps in Tel Aviv and we wanted to catch up with them and see the land of the Bible in one visit. Our trip included a number of social engagements, including cocktails in Tel Aviv and a barbeque on Mount Carmel, which was particularly appropriate when you remember the Old Testament story in which God rained down fire on a bull carcass for Elijah on the same mountain. We, however, lit the fire with a more conventional approach.

At this barbecue, drinks were flowing along with the socializing. I'm sure there were some uninteresting conversations, but I couldn't find one. What I did find was myself in the company of a senior member of the U.S. Marines. His job, he told me, was to train officers in strategy and tactics to equip them for every eventuality in today's troubled world. I listened with fascination as this extremely articulate man explained that his current curriculum involved looking at the lives, methods, and leadership styles of great figures from history. Napoleon, Alexander the Great, Julius Caesar, and a host of others were up for examination. This man was gripped with his subject and I guessed his students were as well. I certainly was too, but after listening for some time I asked him if he had considered examining the methods of a man from history who, after only 36 months of public work, had a current world following of around two billion. He was a man who was born not very far from where we were meeting and spent his 33 years in the same country we were both visiting. I was referring, of course, to Jesus of Nazareth.

There was a pause. "You know," he said, "it never occurred to me to consider him in that way." Graciously, he thanked me for the suggestion and assured me he would follow it up. He promised to approach the subject with an open mind.

That's all I'm asking of you. Run with me and I will help you run with Jesus of Nazareth. But run with an open mind and I promise that you will never race the same way again.

READY? HERE WE GO

I have to confess: I'm a pretty competitive person. When I'm on an exercise machine, I check what the people on either side of me are doing to see if I'm running faster than them as we all go nowhere on our treadmills. My competitive character has led me into numerous sports with varying degrees of success. One thing I have learned is that, in most sports, it is the way you finish that defines your success.

If you don't relate to sports metaphors, try this: The same is true of songwriting – another one of my passions. Having recorded three albums with my band, I have also learned that the musicians, producer, sound engineers, and recording company all work together to create a finished product. And it is how it is finished that determines the nature of the album.

The same is true of a painting, a poem, a book, a project, a construction, a contract... and a life. In this race of rats in which you and I find ourselves, there will be many twists, turns, and challenges. But your success and mine will be defined, whether we like it or not, by how we cross the finish line.

You will not be surprised, then, when I suggest to you that a good – in fact, the best – place to start in learning how to race from Jesus of Nazareth is to have a look at how he finished. In fact, I suggest that this principle of looking at the finish is more true for his finish than most.

For all of us, the way we end reflects the way we have run. The way we die reflects the way we have lived, and the way we face the end shows how we faced the race. But for him, his last hours were without doubt his finest hours. Consider these words: "[Christ's] death is not an incident of his life. It is the aim of it. The laying down of his life is not an accident in his career. It is his vocation; it is that in which the...purpose of his life is revealed."[1]

Remember, we observed earlier that millions of racers race with his symbol around their necks. That symbol is the representation of the place where he spent his last hours. Imagine having a guillotine or an electric chair around your neck as a piece of jewelry. It would be shocking. But this startling habit of the followers of the carpenter indicates that, by wearing a symbol of his last hours, they are pointing to a profound truth.

SEVEN SECRETS

Jesus of Nazareth saw his final hours as the culmination of his life's work. His death was work, literally. Now, you and I might see our work as death, but for him, those final six hours contained his ultimate achievements. This was the time he had been preparing for all his life. Everything pointed here and this was where and when the real job got done. We can and will look at the preceding laps of his race, but if we want to find the golden lessons for our race we must look here first.

And what happens when you look? You will find that he tells you in his own words how he was finishing. He opens windows into his work, his soul, and his race, through which you can look and learn. The sense you will need to use for this learning is your hearing. If you listen, you will hear what he said as he finished. And each sentence he says will show you how he raced – and how *you* can race. More than just a set

---

[1]   James Denney *The Death of Christ* (Eerdmans, 1911), 121.

of rules or a list of ideas, you will discover that he is providing you with a different way to race. He is rescuing you from a stress-filled, self-destructive race, and is giving you energy for running a new type of race altogether. Lily Tomlin famously said, "The trouble with the rat race is that, even if you win, you're still a rat."[2] She's right. But what if you find a different way to run, a different understanding of what it means to winning, and a way to become a rejuvenated rat?

While Jesus of Nazareth was running his very last laps, which lasted 360 minutes, he spoke seven sentences. The seven last sentences he spoke as he literally crossed his finish line can give you profound insight into how he fulfilled his life's mission and purpose and provide you with a perfect model as to how you can fulfill yours. That was the content of my midsummer night's dream. It was a revelation of seven powerful secrets of how to run this rat race.

I have been sharing these secrets with thousands of people over the years and the principles have and do revolutionize the way we work. So, keep your mind open as we explore the secrets together.

Just before I look at the first secret that relates to stress, let me give you a couple of thoughts. Some of you may be hard-working individuals with no particular affiliation to any faith. You may be from a background which is vaguely familiar with the Jesus stories. I have tried to write in such a way that doesn't assume in any way that you are a follower of Jesus. The reason for this is that I am trying to show you how this man who undoubtedly changed the world can change the way you work, whoever you are. Having said that, I will need to quote him and describe him and take what he said at face value. I can promise you that, if you run with me beside him, you will learn helpful

---

2   http://en.thinkexist.com/quotation/the_trouble_with_the_rat-
race_is_that_even_if_you/8038.html

tactics for your race. For others who are already convinced followers, I hope you will see things you have not seen before. These are things that will strengthen your resolve to run the race and finish it well. Besides, you've already decided to run, so why not run a better race?

We are all racing anyway, so let's run together for a while and listen to the expert. Now, let's do something about this stress monster.

LAP ONE:
STRESS REDUCTION –
THE FORGIVING SOUL

You know when stress is affecting your race when your race starts to feel more like a fight. Suddenly there are enemies everywhere and your soul is under threat. At this point, the last thing you want is another to-do list of tasks to perform to reduce your stress, because all that will do is create another item in your inbox fanning the flames of guilt and procrastination.

In my years as a stress consultant, I have discovered that confusion about stress is itself stressful, and that understanding the stress process is a great solvent which clears your head. Any racer will tell you that races are run and won in the mind as much as anywhere else. So to slay this stress monster and defeat your enemy you first have to understand it in your mind.

If I could tell you in three or four words what stress is, I would be a very wealthy racer. People are complex and so are their stresses, but they are not so complex as to defy description.

Some time ago, I was given permission to use a stress assessment questionnaire called the Pressure Management Indicator (the Indicator, for short).[1] It measures 24 aspects of stress and pressure. If you were to answer its questions, you would get a 12-page personal profile that reflects your behavior in relation to your workplace stress. If you were part of a group of 10 or more filling in the Indicator, you could get a group report, sometimes called a stress audit, showing you as a group your stress-related issues.

---

[1] Stephen Williams, *The Indicator* (Resource Systems, 2000).

AN ANCIENT STRESS AUDIT

I would like to introduce to you one such group. They are the main characters involved in the final laps of Jesus' race. I'm going to perform with you a stress audit on these characters and use that to show you the meaning of your stress. Once we've done that, we can then look at how Jesus himself coped with his stress and learn secret one for your race.

The advantage of having a human mind is that you can take your thoughts to anyplace and any time you want and race with your ancestors to learn their secrets. That's what we're going to do now.

Our audit starts at the beginning of the last week of Jesus' life. It is known around the world as Easter Week or Holy Week. The events took place in Israel's capital city of Jerusalem. As we race through Jerusalem together, I ask you to closely observe these characters – how they react, survive, and protect themselves – in short, how they are running. We will then compare their running style with the central runner himself. Above all, listen as you run.

The first moment of our audit takes place just after Jesus arrives in Jerusalem on a donkey to the cheers and chants of the crowd. You can hear their enthusiasm because they see this as a political event which will be the answer to their hopes and dreams. They have placed their trust in this person and his arrival to give them what they wanted. You can almost miss the meaning of this. Let me tell you straight away that, as you race down the road into Jerusalem, you can hear something which will help you understand your own stress.

Ask yourself these questions: On what or whom am I pinning my hopes? What is my dream? This crowd was making a mistake which would come back to punch them in the face. They had misplaced their ideals and invested in the wrong agenda.

RUNNING WITH DREAMS

As we race, we carry dreams in our souls – dreams of meaning, purpose, and achievement. We have something or someone to race for. There is absolutely nothing wrong with that. You cannot live without hopes and dreams. You cannot race without reason. But, and it is a *big* but, be careful what you dream for.

When a hope is dashed or a dream is disappointed, the fragments become the seeds of stress, and frustration follows. Many racers I have run with have lost heart because they were disappointed by the cause in which they believed. The carpenter on the donkey was not going to become the president of Israel and throw out the Romans. He never promised he would. So the cheering crowd has set themselves up for a disappointment, and it will end in jeers. So as you read this, you might consider if what you are living for is worth dying for, and if the purpose of your race is clear. We will come back to this many times. Please bear in mind that shattered dreams are massive stressors. But on the positive side, fulfilled hopes are enormously nourishing. So let's race on.

FINANCIAL SCAMS

On arrival in the capital, a rare scenario unfolds at the central temple. The normally calm and calming carpenter pulls out a whip and furiously expels a whole bunch of foreign exchange dealers from the trading floor they had set up in the vast temple lobby.

To call this provocative behavior would be a massive understatement. But who was he provoking and what would crawl out from underneath the tables? To get the stress lesson here, you need to be aware that a massive financial racket was being run in this part of the city. Money exchange prices were fixed to rake in commissions on official currencies. Pre-endorsed wildlife was being sold at premium rates for specific sacrificial purposes. Any transaction in this closed market generated a profit for a man named Caiaphas and his father in-law Annas. Millions of dollars per year were being skimmed off into their pockets by running this trade. The trading posts were even called the "Booths of Annas."

Not surprisingly, these characters were furious at the carpenter's antics. Their immediate reaction was to plot his downfall. For them to survive, he must not. So they found a willing ally named Judas who was prepared to make a deal. For Annas and Caiaphas Temple Services, Inc., the corporate behavior included crushing opposition. It was their survival strategy. And for your stress insight you can take this next fact into your mind: Stress and corrupt behaviors go hand in hand. Once provoked, these men turned into destroyers.

Right now, you may be suffering at the hands of such people. For them, finance is their cause and money must be made at any human cost. Anyone who challenges them will feel the weight of a financial crunch and may lose their job, their freedom, or their livelihood. This may be the relevant stress lesson for you at this point in your race.

Judas, whose name is synonymous with treachery, may have had another agenda. It was more than likely he was with the chanting crowd in wanting political revolution. Maybe in his mind he had decided that, if he could force Jesus' hand by provoking an open conflict, he could precipitate a revolution. This was another tactic that would end in the destruction of his dreams and his own self. Let's race on.

WORKLOADS, WORKLOADS

Have you ever tried to run, even slowly, while carrying a bag, a case, or a backpack? Depending on your fitness level, you will find this somewhat of a strain. Now, what if you were carrying five bags, or

10? If the weight keeps increasing, you will reach a point where racing becomes almost impossible. This is a description of one of the most commonly reported stressors – workload. Workload-related stress has two components: Work that is too much to do, and work that is too difficult to do. As you experience this, it may even be a combination of the two.

Such was the case all over Jerusalem at the time of this event. There were at least a quarter of a million extra inhabitants in the city for this holiday week. The whole city was groaning under this workload. As a result, people were tired, exhausted, irritable, and easily manipulated. They were not thinking straight. When they came to make their choices at the end of the week – choices that would result in a verdict of execution – they had become reduced to an unthinking group of automatons.

If you are operating in an overloaded, over-burdened context, your own decision-making faculties will be affected. Stress is not just about your own issues. You are in a context. Look around you. There will be clues – tiredness, absenteeism, conflict, impatience, and even high infection rates. If this is the case, you may be in a risky environment.

As you run slowly through this part of Jerusalem you can put this other piece of information into your stress file: Overwork is dangerous. Hard work can lead to death. The melting pot can become too hot and there are some real risks to watch out for here. Let's race on.

PILATE: INDECISION

If you want to run beside Pontius Pilate for a while, don't expect to get too far. Charged by his employers back at global HQ with keeping a lid on an explosive region, this Roman regional governor faced a daunting task. On top of that, he had married into the first family and was related to the Caesars via his wife.

Some racers reading this already relate to his pressure. You have to control a volatile team or company. You have to make strong decisions without full knowledge of a situation. And for some, you realize your family is watching very closely. Race carefully. There may be trouble ahead. And in this case, trouble was directly ahead in the form of the accused carpenter – accused of what, however, was not so easy to figure out.

If you decide one way, you upset the crowd. If you decide the other way, you upset your conscience. If you take this route, you trouble your wife. If you take that other route, you provoke power struggles.

So Pilate is paralyzed and vacillates. He keeps going out and in, turning around in his mind what to do. His wife has had trouble sleeping over this and he was living a nightmare. And you know how he feels. You are now chasing your tail wondering what to do for the best. It's another dimension of stress and can be added to your audit collection.

Pilate decided to wash his hands of the decision. But it doesn't work like that in today's world. Responsibility brings its pressures. In fact, we know from stress research that responsibility over people is more stressful than responsibility over projects. But there is no water which can wash the buck from your hands when it stops with you. Let's race on.

PETER: DON'T MESS WITH ME

Have you ever become so mad at what's happening that you feel like lashing out at the nearest person and doing some serious damage? Race beside one of Jesus' three closest friends for a moment, a man called Peter, and you will find a partner in pain. Faced with a scenario which went against everything he wanted, Peter could no longer contain his emotions. His friend and leader was being taken by treacherous, unfair means to a sham trial. It went against everything Peter believed in, stood for, and wanted. He pulled out a real sword and cut off a real ear of one of the arresting party.

When you race with rage in your soul, you are at very high risk. Stress and rage are closely linked and there are plenty of sparks at work which can ignite your explosive core. File this one under "Important" as you build up your stress portfolio. Ask yourself what tends to trigger your anger. It can be working with someone similar to you who reminds you of yourself and mirrors your behavior. It can be a word or an action which brings back a long-term memory of something which devalued you in the past. It could be that you have become overly suspicious of people's motives and you now see conspiracies in innocent actions. Like Peter, you might get furious when the world doesn't go your way.

In the end, your anger will be an attempt to preserve your sense of worth; it will be about reacting to an apparent violation of your deeply held beliefs; or it will have something to do with what you need. When your worth, beliefs, or needs seem to be under threat, then you will draw your sword – and the next move is into stress. Let's race on.

ABUSE OF POWER

Throughout your race, you will come into contact with people who hold authority over you. Ranging from parents to teachers, from employers to the police, from the government to a big brother – you will meet them all – and your time will be in their hands. They will have a particular ability to trigger your stress.

You can find some of these characters in your race through Jerusalem. Legal authorities put together a trial that was against their own laws in order to neutralize the threat of the carpenter-turned-teacher. Religious authorities organized tricks and cheap shots – all illegal at 11 points of their own laws against Jesus – in order to prove that he was outside of their approved belief system. Political figures, like the vicious and amoral King Herod, used the opportunity to form expedient alliances with the established powers. Everyone was trying to minimize the threat, manipulate events, and maximize their own survival, thus furthering their own vested interests. Unfair, unjust, and corrupt practices combined to produce a toxic cocktail of stressors which were thrown in Jesus' direction.

Maybe even now you are carrying the stains of such abuses of power in your own soul. Memories of unfair dismissal or unjust decision-making haunt your mind and torment your thoughts. It makes your blood boil, or at least simmer, to recall individuals from your past laps who have attempted to manipulate events for their own ends. This is more fuel for the stress fire and will need to be dealt with. But right now, you are just adding it to your collection of understandings.

There are two more groups to examine before your audit is complete and we can consider the carpenter.

The first is a group of anonymous soldiers charged with the task of carrying out the order to finish him off. They performed this task with a vicious and vindictive flair. They didn't have to make it so humiliating and extreme. The sentence itself was serious enough but these men chose to add spite to the verdict.

You will meet such people during your race. For them, getting even is not enough. Annihilation is what they crave. They want to wreak havoc on the opposition, destroy souls, and inflict maximum pain. They are just downright violent. They can even appear to be pleasant, but carry a vengeance and venom in their spirits. They are the bullies, the abusers, and the invaders of your peace and they are massively stressful to deal with. Their agenda is to inflict damage, to create wounds in their victim, adding insults to injuries, and going beyond any reasonable behaviors. You might like to identify such characters you have met – or even times when you have acted like this yourself. Such people are dangerous and should only be approached with care, if at all. With each opportunity to abuse, they react with total enthusiasm beyond natural humanity. File this behavior in the "Dangerous" section, but watch out for such a trend in yourself.

FRIENDS IN NEED

Finally, an apparently hapless group seems to be caught in the cross-fire. Eleven friends of the racer are trying so hard to keep up as the race becomes mad with crazy events. It all seems beyond their control. We know them as "the disciples." They have names like Peter, Jim, and John, and they're just regular guys who find themselves in the middle of a storm.

First they react with confusion. Then they react with tiredness and fall asleep. When the events heat up and their leader is taken, Peter fights and the others run. In a nutshell, you have the entire stress scenario of confusion, exhaustion, anger, and fear. Mix up these ingredients and stress is served.

It's worth noting at this point of the race how important the physical component of stress is. Stress is now implicated in seven out of the top 10 killers in the world.[2] It increases risks of heart disease, strokes, injuries, suicide, and homicides. It is indirectly linked to cancer, chronic liver disease, lung disease, and bronchitis. You feel its effects in your

---

[2] James Quick, *Journal of Occupational Health and Psychology*,
    Vol. 3, No. 4 (1998), 291.

gut, your skin, your headaches, your backaches, and energy levels. The catalogue of physical symptoms associated with stress can include increased infection rates, hormonal disturbances, muscle degeneration, aches and pains, and of course, sleep disturbances. Some people sleep more; others sleep less. Some cry more; others can't cry at all.

The 11 friends who fell asleep in the small olive garden just prior to Jesus' arrest were almost certainly exhausted with the stress of trying to keep up.

Now, let's pause for a moment and run in place while I show you the meaning of stress from your stress audit.

DEFINING STRESS - FIVE QUESTIONS

The key to understanding and therefore reducing stress is to realize that stress is a reaction. Stress professionals talk about "the stress response." Once you see this key you can begin to turn it to your advantage.

All the characters in first-century Jerusalem were reacting. You can run back and have a look if you want. You'll notice that they plotted, schemed, vacillated, cheered, raged, fell asleep, lashed out, and conspired. The list is endless. Once you realize that stress is a reaction, you will be in a position to scrutinize its characteristics. To do this, ask yourself five key questions.

First question: *Whose reaction is it?* Run back again if you need, but the players in the Jerusalem drama had names – Peter, Annas, Pontius, and so on. Their reactions to the pressures of Jerusalem and this troublesome carpenter were all very personal. Each character responded in his or her unique way. Whose reaction is it? Yours. This is why two people can encounter the same event and react completely differently. "Two men look through their prison bars, as the rhyme goes. One sees the jail; one sees the stars." Stress is about your personal reaction. Therefore, stress reduction will include understanding more and more about your own personality and your individual reactions. That's why there are more learning laps to be run in this book. (See laps three and five.)

Second question: *What kind of reaction is it?* The answer here may be complex, but if you look back through the streets of Jerusalem you will find that the reactions generally become more and more heated as the week wears on. The frustration builds up and things start to boil over. The stress reaction is almost always an angry reaction. The anger may not be rage, it may be quite silent – almost despair – but an element of frustration is almost always found deep at the core. So you might like to ask what you are angry about at work. Like Peter, you feel as if you want to draw your sword, but you can't. What kind of reaction is it? Well, it's usually an angry one. So for stress reduction you will need to understand why you are angry and what you are angry about. Hang on, we're not done yet.

Third question: *Where does this reaction take place?* We've looked at Jerusalem in the first century, but we could also look at London, Paris, New York, Beijing, Bangkok, Moscow, or Lagos in the twenty-first century. The city is not the place, it's the people in the place. The reactions were showing themselves in people's thoughts (plotting, scheming, organizing), people's feelings (shouting, drawing swords), and in their bodies (falling asleep, having dreams). The reaction shows itself in your mind, your feelings, and your body. So stress reduction may well include issues around diet, exercise, and relaxation, but beware of fixing the symptoms without looking at the root issues.

Fourth question: *Why are you reacting?* Each character in our audit had an agenda. In fact, they all had the same agenda – survival. This survival agenda included self-interest, self-promotion, and an attempt to succeed. For the temple moguls, survival and success was about financial success. For the friends who ran away, it was about not being arrested and maintaining personal safety. For Herod, it was about sycophantic power. The fact is, we're all just trying to make it. The stress reaction is our attempt to use what we can to make it, by fair means or foul. The stress reduction issue will revolve around figuring out what it means to survive and thrive. What does real success actually consist of? (See lap three.) It will involve thinking about matters of identity and worth.

Fifth question: *What are you reacting to?* Look over your shoulder back in Jerusalem and you will see a man, a donkey, a whip, a quarter of a million visitors, a crowd, and every conceivable group dynamic. What was each person reacting to? The answer? It could be anything. The trigger for a stress reaction can be anything at all. A word, an action, an event, a memory, a thought – anything you name. The stress build-up starts when something happens. The build-up completes when it results in anger, showing itself in your mind, your feelings, and your body.

If you want a clue as to what kind of triggers are most common, I suggest you consider the word, "change." You can rephrase the words, "something happens" to "something changes," and suddenly you are in stress territory. So how do you react to change? The change doesn't have to be bad. For example, promotion is usually seen as a good thing, but it is still a change and carries a stress warning. The carpenter's arrival in Jerusalem changed everything. He didn't just overturn the tables. He overturned ideas, power bases, moral codes, legal and religious rules, ancient conventions, and established behaviors. In short, this one man was a walking pressure dispenser. His arrival disturbed the counterfeit peace that was created by the corrupt conspirators in the city and challenged them to face up to change. This they did not like. Not at all. Trouble was inevitable.

If you put together the lessons from your stress audit, you can come up with a clear description of stress. Stress is a reaction. Stress is *my* reaction. Stress is an *angry* reaction. Stress takes place in my mind, my feelings, and my body, and it is connected to change. So if you want a working definition, here it is:

Stress is my angry mental, emotional, and physical reaction to internal or external change.

There is one absolutely crucial insight which will help you clarify stress here. Note that I have described change as either internal or external. Let me explain.

STRESS AND YOUR BIG BRAIN

You and I are very clever humans. We may be in a rat race but we are members of the human race. As such, you have the ability to use your massive brain to generate all kinds of thoughts, ideas, and beliefs. What does this mean for stress? Quite simply, it means that you not only react to things that are happening, but also what you *think* is happening. In other words, you can react to your own perceptions. When the carpenter arrived on the donkey, the crowd saw a freedom fighter and the temple authorities saw a financial threat. The children in the crowd probably just saw the donkey. In those moments, each person was formulating an idea or a belief about what they saw, and then they reacted to that belief.

This is our unique blessing and curse at the same time. You can react to your own interpretation of events which may or may not be accurate.

Consider two employees. The boss arrives and announces he wants to meet with each one, individually, for an hour during the morning. One employee thinks, "Great, I have been trying to get an hour with him for ages. I have some new ideas I want to bounce around. We can have a coffee and go through them, spark some ideas, and come up with a plan that I will really enjoy implementing."

The other employee thinks, "Great. Now I'm in trouble. There either must be some issue that has gone wrong, or he wants to give me a whole lot of new work, which will ruin my week. Or, worse still, maybe he wants to fire me."

What just happened? Same boss, same comment, but each employee chose to believe different interpretations of the event. One is exhilarated, while the other is angry and stressed.

In fact, the boss wanted to seek some advice on a proposal received from a consulting firm and wanted two other perspectives to help him make up his mind. So they were both wrong.

Consider these two observations:

*"Everything is what your opinion makes of it, and that opinion
is within yourself."*
– Marcus Aurelius (Roman emperor, AD 170)[3]

"People are disturbed not by things, but the views they take of them."
– Epictetus (philosopher, AD 55-135)

These ancient observations are vital in your understanding of modern stress. You and I can manufacture beliefs in almost any situation and then react to those beliefs. For example, consider suspicion. Someone says something pleasant and you react by doubting their motives, thinking they want something from you. You become irritated at the

---

[3]   Marcus Aurelius, *Mediations* (Everyman's Library, 1946).

fact that they want something from you. Here comes stress.

So you might like to ask yourself what you believe about events at work. The bad news about your ability to generate such thoughts is that it greatly increases your repertoire of stress reactions. The good news is that you can do something about it.

STRESS BEYOND BELIEF

You can stop running in place now, because we're going to race out of Jerusalem to a hill not far from the city wall. Here you can see that a man who started the week as the source of pressure has now become the person under unimaginable stress and pressure.

It's hard to think of anything more stressful than being crucified. First, nails are hammered through your wrists and ankles. Then you're hoisted up between earth and sky on a wooden structure and jolted into position. You are left for hours to a slow, thirst-ridden, asphyxiating, agonizing death. They say the rhythm of crucifixion is characterized by the victim hoisting himself up on torn and gashed limbs to get into a position to breathe, and then collapsing under his own body weight, time and time again, until there is simply no strength left to live. To shorten the torture, sometimes the pitiful sequence was stopped by the breaking of legs in order to remove the ability to rise up and breathe.

Such was the fate of Jesus of Nazareth. Prior to these hours, he had been flogged, beaten, and abused by the world's expert executioners, the Romans. His ordeal lasted six hours. They did indeed come to break his legs, but found him already dead. So they thrust a spear into his ribcage to be sure. Stitched up by religious, civil, and military authorities alike, he now had found himself condemned to die between two criminals outside the walls of the city they called holy – Jerusalem.

We are not racing to this spot to observe a tragedy or to feel pity. We are here to learn. As you listen, you can hear the first words he spoke as this period of incomprehensible pressure began, "Father, forgive them, for they do not know what they are doing."[4] In the stress-laden atmosphere, this line is a breath of fresh air. There had been a discordant sound echoing throughout the week coming from crowds, kings, governors, lawyers, friends, enemies, and soldiers. Now there is this altogether different note.

Stress, you will recall, is a reaction or a response. Here you have the carpenter's response to the events of the week and the hours of this day. Of all the options open to him, he chooses words of forgiveness. You can be sure the words were chosen very carefully – he knew they would be among his last. And from his own story, he had been preparing for this all his life.

So here you can capture the key stress management skill that will enable you to react in a life-enhancing manner, rather than with self-destruction. This skill of forgiveness was not just brought out of a closet for this moment; it was his lifestyle and central message. "Forgive us our sins, for we also forgive everyone who sins against us,"[5] was at the heart of his model prayer. Turning the other cheek, writing off debts, sending people away with no condemnation in their souls – these were all features of his approach.

Ancient wisdom it may be, but listen to writer and philanthropist Hannah Moore: "Forgiveness is the economy of the heart. ... Forgiveness saves the expense of anger, the cost of hatred, the waste of

---

4   Luke 23:34

5   Luke 11:4

spirits."[6] I would add to that, "...*and the surcharge of stress.*"

Stress, as we have seen, is closely related to anger and frustration. It is the build-up of fiery energy in your soul which starts to consume you from within. Designed to give you energy to cope with rising demands, the stress response can quickly turn toxic, poisoning your thoughts, feelings, and body. By contrast, forgiveness "warms the heart and cools the sting."[7]

Forgiveness is a powerful, complicated skill which can take years to develop, especially if you have grown up in an unforgiving environment.

But here in this horrific pain that we cannot imagine, Jesus of Nazareth gives the stress message for the racing rat. Rather than rage, forgive. Rather than destroy, forgive. Rather than take out your sword, forgive. Rather than manipulate, forgive.

All the moves of the players in the preceding week's deadly game were out-maneuvered by this reaction of forgiveness. This is not the last gasp of a pitiful, broken man – there is great power here. The great advocate of peace, Mahatma Gandhi, explained that, "The weak can never forgive; forgiveness is the attribute of the strong."[8] And years later, Indira Gandhi, India's great woman prime minister, observed, "Forgiveness is a virtue of the brave."[9]

So as you race, you will find yourself in situations where there is

---

[6] http://thinkexist.com/quotation/forgiveness_is_the_economy_of_the_heart/209023.html

[7] William Arthur Ward http://en.thinkexist.com/quotation/forgiveness_is_a_funny_thing-it_warms_the_heart/8446.html

[8] Prabhu and Rao, ed., *Mind of Mahatma Ghandi*, 3rd Edition (1968).

[9] http://thinkexist.com/quotation/forgiveness_is_a_virtue_of_the_brave/261485.html

high risk of damage. Other racers will bump you and knock you off course. But the real battle will be inside of you, as you attempt to manage, control, and cope with your reactions. Then the question becomes, is it possible to keep turning stress into forgiveness, as the carpenter did?

THE FORGIVING SOUL

When I studied for my master's degrees in stress management, I came across a number of multi-disciplinary academic approaches that were new to me. There were psychologists who specialized in spirituality, mental health professionals studying religion, along with a whole variety of job titles so long as to be unpronounceable.

To my further surprise, a number of these leading researchers had taken a good, long, hard look at forgiveness.[10] Among other revelations, they outlined a four-stage approach to forgiveness that I have found very helpful in my own race.

The first stage is an admission of hurt or injury. Have you ever seen someone with a red face and clenched fists, breathing hard and saying through gritted teeth, "I am not angry!"? Everything about them except their words tells you that they are, most definitely, angry.

Some years ago, I was bullied at work. It was an unpleasant devaluing experience that wounded me deeply. Two years after the events, I was speaking with a counselor friend of mine and recalling the episode. He turned to me and said, "You're still hurting about this aren't you?" And I replied, "Yes, I am." This was a breakthrough moment for me.

---

[10] Kenneth Pargament, PhD and Carl Thoresen, PhD, *Forgiveness: Theory, Research, and Practice*, ed. Michael McCullough, PhD (Guilford Press, 2000).

I must admit that it was also a bit of an embarrassment, because I teach, lecture, and train on these issues, and here I was grappling with something I had held onto for two years.

But there can be no forgiveness if there is no recognition of hurt. Once you admit you are hurting, you move into a place of truth and light, and can at least begin to move forward in your race. Without this recognition, you will race with a limp.

The second stage of forgiveness is a commitment to forgive. Martin Luther King described forgiveness as, "an attitude, not an occasional act."[11] Others have observed that forgiveness is not an action after the fact but an attitude with which you enter each moment. A look through this window into the racing technique of Jesus of Nazareth reveals a lifestyle driven by the motivation to forgive. It is everywhere in his teaching, his personal encounters, and his manner.

If your personal value system is saturated with a forgiving attitude, when you are hurt and admit it, you will soon connect with your commitment to forgive. This connection is only part of the journey to full forgiveness, but it is vital. To forgive, you have to believe in forgiveness. To forgive requires an intentional movement in that direction. This observation is important because, if you are honest, forgiveness is a very demanding decision. You can be in so much pain that you feel paralyzed in the face of forgiveness. The last thing you want added to your emotional baggage at this point is a case labeled, "Guilt." There is nothing wrong with being in this *commitment* stage. It is a lap you have to run. Some personality types run it very quickly. Most, however, need much more time. This is where stage three sets in.

---

[11] http://thinkexist.com/quotation/forgiveness-is-not-an-occasional-act-it-is-an/538162.html

If you have recognized your hurt and are committed to forgive, you will need a time of thinking, reflecting, and mulling over what has happened. You will need to review what you did, what others did, and why it happened. You will have questions and deep thoughts to explore. What has happened may have dredged up an old memory or past hurt. You may be dealing with the pain of betrayal or being misunderstood.

In the Jerusalem audit, you can see the full repertoire of hurt that led to the moment that we are examining. Betrayed and deserted by his own team. Misinterpreted and misunderstood by acquaintances and the public alike. Maligned and slandered by his accusers. Mocked by soldiers, physically abused, mentally violated, and emotionally assaulted – he had run the gauntlet of human insults. It is in the time of reflection and analysis that you replay what you have been through and attempt to make some sense of it. You are complex. Your hurts are complex. You cannot just snap your fingers and make hurts disappear. You can't nail them in a box or still their voices. You need to engage with the army of anxieties that assault your soul.

Again, some personalities can do this very quickly. Others, probably most of us, take longer. But the pace doesn't matter, because reflection is a real stage, and is itself part of the forgiveness process.

If you know the famous story of Joseph (of *Technicolor Dream Coat* fame) – the dreamer who became a slave, the slave who became a servant, the servant who became a prisoner, and the prisoner who became prime minister of Egypt – you will remember that, at the beginning of this story, he was thrown into a pit by his jealous brothers. Then, at the end of the story, he is somehow able to say, "You intended this for evil, but God intended it for good."[12] But I doubt that, the

---

[12] Genesis 50:19

moment they threw him into the pit, he looked up with mercy in his eyes and was able to say those words. It was only years later that he could manage it. He needed stage three, a time to reflect, as part of his forgiveness process.

Stage four is when your choice actually bears fruit. Lewis Smedes observed, "You will know that forgiveness has begun when you recall those who hurt you and feel the power to wish them well."[13] This is the time when you can love your enemies and bless those who hurt you. This is the time when you have made deep and profound choices and will no longer hold onto your anger or bitterness. You now experience the freedom from resentment and are able to simply let it go.

This, dear racer, is the key stress management skill. If you can keep dropping your baggage of anger, resentment, frustration, and bitterness as you run, you will reduce, and in some cases, eliminate unnecessary stress from your race. Note that I said *unnecessary* stress. You will already know that some stress is necessary. The energy to perform, to rise to a challenge, and meet a deadline contains an element of stress. But it is the toxic, fiery element which turns healthy stress into distress and provokes destruction.

HURDLES

This rat race not only involves examining baggage which you may need to drop, but it includes hurdles which you need to jump. Overcoming stress with forgiveness throws up some such hurdles. It is worth looking at them and learning to jump them. Like so much of this race, these hurdles are in the mind.

---

[13] http://thinkexist.com/quotation/you_will_know_that_forgiveness_has_begun_ when_you/214404.html

The first hurdle is illustrated by the statement, "I will not forgive until he/she apologizes (or asks for forgiveness, or admits a mistake, etc., etc., etc.)." Let's label it the *forgiveness-pending* hurdle. To clear it, you will need to take a mental leap. Ask yourself these questions: What if they never apologize? What if they never admit it?

If you stop at the forgiveness-pending hurdle, you make yourself hostage to other racers' behavior and you come to a halt. Your anger remains, the toxicity spreads, and you are left with a bitter demeanor. You cannot wait for someone else to make a move – it's your move. The carpenter on the cross didn't wait for anyone to apologize – he forgave.

The second hurdle is that of the *repeat offender* – the same person doing the same thing over and over again. How many times should you forgive? Peter, the swordsman we met earlier, asked Jesus this exact question, suggesting that seven would be a fair number. The reply he got was a larger number, 490![14] The exaggerated point was well-made – this forgiveness is a constant attitude, not a one-off action. This doesn't mean that you never challenge the offender or that you can't take steps to avoid such people. Both are valid racing techniques. If you are working with someone who consistently and constantly causes you grief, you can legitimately and legally challenge them. You can also, in certain cases, avoid them, even choosing to change employment as a stress-management action. But for your well being, you will still need to do this work of forgiveness. Otherwise, the stress will move with you.

There is a third hurdle that will block your lane and needs to be negotiated. This concerns a rising feeling that the offender does not deserve forgiveness and that, if you do forgive, they get away with it.

---

[14] Matthew 18:21-22

This sometimes includes a desire for revenge or getting even. Call it the *revenge* hurdle if you wish. There are a number of pointers that will help you clear this hurdle. First of all, if you think that, by not forgiving someone, you are somehow punishing them, you will soon discover that you are in fact punishing yourself. The stress toxins will stay with you and your health and well-being will be affected.

Secondly, you will be attempting to put yourself in the position of judge, jury, and executioner, but almost certainly without all the evidence. Your desire may be for revenge, but you run a severe risk of overdoing it.

This book is about learning from the master racer, who at so many points could have chosen to fight, run, stand on his rights, or even call on supernatural sources, but he stayed his course and followed through with his mission. He was not going to let the corruption, poor practice, and moral compromise around him stop him from fulfilling his life's purpose. This is a profound learning point. If you divert your energy into revenge, vindictiveness, or spite, you will miss out on your vocation, be deflected from your purpose, and lose your way. Stress and anger are great consumers of resources, and you cannot let them rule your race. The carpenter was going to fulfill his vocation, no matter how others behaved. This is powerful stress management. But it is not the whole story.

SELF HELP VS. OUTSIDE HELP

A number of years ago, while directing a training center and leading a church, I formed a partnership with the national government and ran life-skills training courses for long-term unemployed individuals in order to help them get back into the marketplace. Stress, anger, and frustration management were part of the curriculum, as was learning about forgiveness. A number of course members explained to us that, although they thought this whole approach was valid, there were, they felt, times when they just couldn't do it. They felt that it was just too hard in certain circumstances to practice such principles.

As trainers, we gave them two responses. First, we showed them that they could do much more than they realized by just understanding the stress response and the techniques of thinking and behavior for reducing stress. Secondly, however, we agreed with them that there were times when you could reach your limits. We then arranged an extra-curricular session to share with them our personal approaches to these issues.

This brings us to the underlying nature of this first secret contained in the saying of the carpenter. The phrase is a prayer. It is a request for outside help and power. Because, you see, there comes a point where self-help stops and outside help is needed.

Over the last years, much research has been done concerning prayer in particular, and spirituality in general. Physiologists have noticed the impact of meditation on heart rate, life expectancy and relaxation. Some have attempted to measure the effectiveness of prayer in relation to hospital heart-surgery patients.[15]

Books have been written about spiritual intelligence, articles created about the "God spot" in the brain, and comments made about the value of prayer. Edward Hallowell, a senior lecture at Harvard Medical School and founder-director of the Center for Cognitive and Emotional Health, recommends that "connectedness" is an antidote to some of our worries. He describes it as, "opening up to other people, to other

---

[15] Russell Stannard, *The God Experiment* (Faber and Faber, 1999).

ideas, and to our spiritual side."[16]

You may already be a convinced pray-er, or you may have severe doubts (or both), but whatever your view, you can see that the man who changed the world turned to prayer as a default reaction under pressure. To learn the lessons for your race, it would be worth having a look at this.

The whole phrase under scrutiny was a prayer, but this first word, "father," defines the type of prayer. This word, father, speaks of issues of identity. Jesus saw his own identity in relation to his father, and in so doing he is showing us some strategic skills for stress management.

Ask yourself this question: Where do I get my sense of identity and worth from? If you race back to your Jerusalem audit, you will discover that the ancient racers share common characteristics with their modern counterparts. They got their sense of identity and worth from power, accumulated wealth, or status. When these were threatened, their whole sense of identity was threatened, and they lashed out.

When you go into the marketplace, you will inevitably experience devaluing moments. Bypassed for promotion, overlooked by colleagues, or ignored by a manager, you may find yourself experiencing rising stress levels. But what if your primary sense of identity and worth was independent of such pressures? Suppose you were able to conclude that your worth was derived from the person who made you and who has valued you – God Himself. No one, then, could take that sense of value away.

The implications of this thinking for your work-related stress issues

---

[16] Edward M. Hallowell, M.D., *Worry: When Life is More Scary Than It Should Be* (Random House, October 1997).

are enormous. Within yourself, you can carry an internal sense of worth that is derived from your connectedness to the power of your creator and rescuer. This will create resilience in your being, which will preserve your stability in an unstable, volatile, or hostile market.

So the carpenter's prayer is pointing you to a way of seeing your worth as immune to the market. Let's not be naïve here. Of course finance, status, and security matter, but only in a secondary sense. If you allow them to become primary, you will open yourself up to threats, damage, and stress.

On another note, this prayer is also an indication of security. Where do you get your sense of security from? Your brain, your savings, your company, your family? The carpenter's prayer is a prayer of trust. He is taking a risk by counting on his father as the one in whose hands his present and future lies.

If you equate security with your own assets, when those assets dwindle, your security evaporates. If you take the same position of this prayer, which is modeled during these six hours of dying, you discover that security is also a spiritual matter that reaches beyond the immediate images you see.

Lastly, this prayer is a prayer of values. Jesus used his understanding of the father's ways to calibrate his actions in the human race. In order to develop the wisdom to race, he studied, watched, and listened for those values and behaviors that were in harmony with the father's expressed wishes. Here again your race can be revolutionized by the carpenter's prayer. How do you decide what is right, wrong, or wise? Everyone is looking for a moral code or compass, and this prayer points to a spiritual direction and connects with another stress-reducing resource.

Lack of a sense of security or absence of an ethical framework can be enormously stressful. The father prayer erodes the enormity of this stress by pouring powerful solutions onto the hard issues.

Whether you are a default pray-er or an interested observer, you will need to find your sense of identity, worth, security, and values from somewhere. I'm advocating that this carpenter's race *is* that somewhere.

WHO ARE THESE PEOPLE?

There is one last look you can take through this window before we summarize and race on. It focuses on the "them" who Jesus mentions in his words, "Father, forgive *them* for they do not know what they are doing." For him, they were the characters who we have already met in your audit. But who are *your* "them," and how will understanding and identifying them help you race more healthily?

To introduce you to "them," let me tell you a bit about your past. Sometime, not long after you were born, a word crept into your family's vocabulary with increasing regularity. It was a word you heard just when you were about to put your fingers onto something too hot, too cold, too canine, too electrical, or too expensive. It was a word spoken before you ran onto a highway, into a river, or off a cliff. It echoed through your house as you were about to put something unpleasant in your mouth. That word was "No!" It's not that your family was cruel; it was simply that the message, "Don't do that," or "Don't be that," had to be put in place for your safety.

As you ran your teenage laps, other voices said, "Don't wear that, wear this," or "Buy this and be cool," or "Drink this and smoke this". These peer voices now competed with, and often drowned out, your parents' words. Added to these are the voices from TV, magazines, and a million commercials, and there is now a raging chorus of advice, commands, and shouts in your mind. If you attended church or a youth club, other moral and ethical rules would have been put into the mix as well.

The result for you is that, inside your soul, there is an *ideal* you. A you who is a bit taller, a bit shorter, a bit better-looking, a bit wealthier, cleverer, successful, and a you who doesn't really make mistakes.

Unfortunately, residing in your same soul is a *real* you – who messes up, makes mistakes, doesn't get things right, feels awkward, can't dance brilliantly, and harbors a few self-doubts.

The stress implications of this emerge when these two "yous" conflict with each other. Specifically, this shows itself when the ideal you becomes critical, un-accepting, and even angry at the real you. Depending on the severity of the conflict, you can run the risk of living with guilt, anxiety, self-loathing, and ending up as a walking civil war.

Many, many individuals race with internal conflict, which manifests itself in a multitude of marketplace behaviors. The perfectionist who is so hard on himself and others that there he leaves no room for human error. The co-worker who will always blame herself, even if the problem had nothing to do with her. The irritable manager who flies off the handle with the simplest provocation. All these characters are at war with themselves.

What needs to happen here is for the real and ideal aspects to make peace, via an internal forgiveness strategy, to allow the authentic you to emerge. So the chief character in your cast of "them" is really…you. You can test your condition by standing in front of a mirror and asking yourself, "Do I accept who I see?" This will measure your self-acceptance level and give you some insight into your challenge.

Like my life-skills course members, there is much you can do with your built-in resources to re-think your attitude of yourself and develop a more forgiving, realistic relationship in your mind. But also like them, you will reach a limit where you will need, through prayer, to call on the one who specializes in forgiveness and ask him to teach you how to follow the path of the great commandment, which encourages you to "love yourself."[17]

Undoubtedly, your "them" will also include characters who act like a mirror in your life and reflect aspects of yourself that you don't like. They remind you of yourself. Alongside them will be those whose style, personality, or actions remind you of past injuries and connect new anger and stress with old memories. Your "father forgive them" racing style will need to keep these people in view along with a whole host of others who have, or had, power and influence in your life.

It's worth mentioning two such people. Let me illustrate. Some time ago, I was approached by a young woman who was having trouble with her boss. I knew her boss quite well, so I wondered what the trouble could be. It turned out that she felt un-affirmed, undervalued, and somewhat patronized at work. This surprised me, as the person I knew as her boss was fairly encouraging, as bosses go.

In the course of the conversation, it emerged that her own father had been extremely un-attentive, insensitive, and neglectful of her as she grew up. It became clear that she was looking to her boss to make up this deficiency in her life. Unfortunately, even a good boss cannot do that. She had accidentally brought expectations to work that were doomed to disappointment. She had inadvertently set herself up for a fall. She is not alone. There are large numbers of individuals in all types of work who feel this type of stress. Frustrated at the apparent uncaring nature of their employers, they miss the fact that they are

---

[17] "Love your neighbour as yourself...." Mark 12:30-32

looking for a lost legacy.

A second expression of this syndrome shows itself when someone brings unresolved anger towards either parent to work with them and reacts strongly whenever an employer or senior colleague reminds them of that parental behavior. Résumés are littered with resignations or dismissals that have their roots in unfinished family business.

So the forgiveness challenge is to deal with this legacy. Your parents, or the adults who brought you up, made accidental, or maybe even deliberate, mistakes. I must tell you that the carpenter on the cross is calling you to let them go and run without that terrible legacy on your shoulders.

Generally speaking, the closer someone is to you, the greater the potential there is for pleasure and pain. So to practice forgiveness as a stress-management skill towards these immediate fellow racers is vital for your own career.

THE END OF THE AUDIT

What more can you do with your stress audit? Stress-management professionals talk about different levels of intervention. If a marketplace issue is long working hours and low staffing levels, then a first-level intervention means reducing hours, re-writing job specifications, and employing more people. A second-level intervention will involve helping people to manage their thoughts, feelings, actions, workloads, and reactions more skillfully by training, advice, and example. A third-level intervention involves counseling or medical help for someone in serious trouble.

The carpenter on the cross was operating on all these levels. He saw his work as a global rescue plan, providing the means for the reconfiguration of structures around freedom, justice, and forgiveness. His words and behavior provide the model and the insight to empower you to manage stress through forgiveness and complex prayer. Over the years, many racers have experienced the healing power of his work and words when they have found themselves in need of a counselor, friend, or physician.

The Jerusalem audit revealed that no one at the time realized what was actually happening. They saw the events but missed their meaning. They played their part but did not understand the story. They were so consumed with their own agenda that they were blind to the big picture and the implications of their actions. In short, they had no idea what they were doing. Which is why Jesus included the words, "they don't know what they do" in his prayer.

I am continually inviting you to distance yourself from the crowd and see what is actually happening so you can race with the expert and capture his secrets. As we run together, you will find yourself hearing more words as the hours of this Jerusalem day proceed. For now, the father prayer and the forgiveness skill combine to form the first secret on the table.

Actress and comedian Lily Tomlin once said, "Forgiveness means giving up all hope of a better past."[18] She's right. It's time to move away from the past, determine to be defined as a forgiving soul, and explore the power of hope – our next racing secret.

---

[18] http://thinkexist.com/quotation/forgiveness_means_giving_up_all_hope_ for_a_better/344488.html

LAP TWO:
THE POWER OF HOPE –
WHISPERS OF PARADISE

We don't know much about him, but I would like to introduce you to a racer who gives us a tantalizing glimpse into our own hearts. We would know nothing about him at all had he not overlapped with the carpenter as they both crossed the finish line. We don't have his name, or his biography; we only know something of his mental journey and his aspirations. So let's start with what we do know.

Some time in his past, this racer's race had gone wrong. For any one of a range of reasons, he had strayed off the track. Although he had undoubtedly made unwise choices, for which he was responsible, he had not lived the life he had wanted and it had not turned out the way he would have wished. To put it mildly, he was disappointed with himself and his life's course.

Even the most successful, satisfied and high-achievers among us have phases when disappointment creeps in. Single-minded business winners celebrate their trophies but regret their absence at family functions. Aspiring academics enjoy their knowledge but will regret some of the missed moments of enlightenment that they overlooked.

Physically, many racers run with a sense of loss as the aging process and aching limbs remind them of the passing of years – not to mention the passing of faster rats. On a more serious scale, some of you look back on your race so far and see it littered with disappointment, loss, and regret. There are things you should have done but didn't, and things you didn't do that you should have done. You have said mistimed words or taken actions which, if you could, you would unsay and undo.

The middle laps of your race are often those in which some soul-searching reflection causes you to conclude that things did not turn out the way you had expected. Most of us just live with a certain level of disappointment. It may not be debilitating or paralyzing, but merely a faint echo of wistful thoughts that blow through your mind in unguarded moments. Regardless, they remind you of that which might have been.

NOTICE ME

The second item we know about our mysterious man is that he had a profound longing to be noticed, affirmed, and validated. In a world that has a talent for ignoring the individual, forgetting feelings, and devaluing others in order to promote self-interest, this man literally cried out for recognition. And we do too.

From the moment of your birth to the closing of your eyes in death, you carry this longing in your soul. It is not a weakness or a defect; it is a fundamental human trait that's hardwired into your circuitry. It surfaces when you encounter a telephone system that invites you to press number after number to select options as you respond to a recorded voice. It bursts out of you when you find yourself lost in a crowd of co-workers, customers, or competitors and leaps into your mind whenever you feel taken for granted, used, abused, or ignored. When your cherished ideas or dreams are crushed or your rites of passage are forgotten, or when your feelings are hurt or your talents are undervalued, you join voices with this man who occupied the place of execution right next to Jesus of Nazareth, and cry out, "Remember me!"

This man was the thief crucified beside Jesus. At that moment during crucifixion, his memories, hopes, fears, mistakes, and feelings had all been pinned to a piece of wood with him, hanging there naked in public. He was exposed for what he was – just a person like you and me.

You undoubtedly share much in common with this enigmatic individual, and in other ways you may be quite different to him. But the reason we are connecting with him at all is that the more we get inside his experience, the more we will be able to view the carpenter on the adjacent cross. This will help us glimpse something of the carpenter's momentous race from a unique, close-up perspective. As we capture this view, you will be able to learn lessons for your race which will connect you with a powerful source of hope.

REAL, BUT NOT EASY

These will not be easy moments – none of the real ones are – but they will be meaningful. And if you are prepared to take this a step at a time we can plot a path together to a better place.

To engage with the interaction that transpired under these unusual circumstances, you will be well advised to start with the observation that, for some considerable time, Jesus had said nothing at all to this convicted criminal hanging next to him. In fact, Jesus didn't initiate the exchange that we are examining – he responded to the words put to him.

Throughout his short race, Jesus had been leading by example, using a language of actions and reactions in response to others. His motivations were clearly apparent to any observant onlooker. This, of course, is what our thief was doing – watching and listening. Thieves are good at that.

What he saw and heard was startling. He had seen a man who was treated with vindictive spite by soldiers and who was so exhausted on the way to the execution site that they had hauled someone out of the crowd to carry the cross for him. The thief had heard the shouts and screams of women who were grief-stricken at the thought of this miscarriage of justice. He had listened to the comments of the carpenter who had told them not to mourn for him but for the disastrous future which was coming their way. Our thief had seen them place a plaque with an ironic inscription labeling him as "KING" while they set about annihilating him. Even for a criminal who had been around the block a few times, these were puzzling events to compute. But he kept watching and listening.

You might want to note at this point, in your own thinking, that the people close to you right now are watching you. They are observing how you race, taking in what happens to you and logging your reactions. Before you even say a word to them, they have already heard your life and watched how you race.

So we have the carpenter at work in view, and the thief immediately beside him. We are witnesses to a conversation. Remember, the carpenter saw these hours as the climax of the work he had been born to do. We are watching someone engage with a very intentional person right next to him, and that carpenter is at work. Whatever you learn or see in this exchange will be applicable to the exchanges you have with people right next to you – your peers, colleagues, team members, or co-workers.

Let me quote you the two sentences which passed between these men as their lives drew to a close:

Criminal One: *"Jesus, remember me when you come into your kingdom."*
Jesus of Nazareth: *"I tell you the truth, today you will be with me in paradise."*[1]

We will soon explore the specific content and meaning of these words, but to discover secret two on your race, you will need to capture the overall spirit of them. The thief makes a request and the carpenter gives

---

[1]   Luke 23:43

him a response. The request, as we have seen, comes from a disappointed, desperate man who probably deserved what he was getting. The response, however, is somewhat surprising.

THE LAST SURPRISE

Whatever its exact meaning, the response is a sentence of hope, good news, and enormous encouragement. To capture the spirit of the response, you must notice that there is no hint of condemnation or criticism. It is unrelentingly positive. There is no scrutiny of the criminal's résumé and blemished record. There is no rebuke or reprimand. There is no hint of superiority or suspicion. In fact, there is a disarmingly generous and gracious flavor to the reply.

Underneath these words is an essential foundation without which life is impossible. Jesus transmits to him the most powerful energy known to the human race – the energy of encouragement. *With* encouragement, you can start, go on, keep-going, continue, and eventually finish. *Without* encouragement, you stumble, fall, slow-down, atrophy, dwindle, and die.

Take this moment to consider the power of encouragement and the necessity of hope. In the marketplace, there is a proud boast from many strong self-made successful racers. They say something like, "I tell it like it is." Behind this motto is a belief that we must face the reality of things as they actually are without pulling any punches or burying any part of our anatomy in the sand.

Comedy writer Robert Orben observed, "We have enough people who tell it like it is – now we could use a few who tell it like it can be."[2] It may be meant as a joke, but he's touching on the power of hope and encouragement.

Take your mind back to a conversation when you were on the receiving end of sustained and detailed encouragement. How did it feel? What did it do to you? You could almost touch the energy it gives you and the exhilaration that rushes through your veins. It lifts you up and quickens your pace, giving you a genuine sense of well-being and pleasure. It can bring a smile to your face or a blush to your cheeks. Whatever your overall reaction, you have to admit: it feels good.

Jesus of Nazareth created a climate of encouragement and hope wherever he went. People who were physically damaged or destroyed found restoration. Women who had been manipulated, abused, or despised found acceptance and respect. Crowds found a speaker who could take them out of themselves and into a different order of things that was full of surprises and puzzles. And anyone who was rejected by the group found recognition in his eyes. He specialized in spotting the outsiders and bringing them in. He found the left-behind and helped them catch up. He soothed the burnt-out who needed a rest.

This is what was happening in this brief exchange. The thief who knew all about criticism, condemnation, and rejection, because he had lived with it all his life, discovered an affirming, accepting promise from the person right by his side.

---

[2] Cited by Franzy Fleck in *What Successful Principals Do!* (Eye On Education, February 8, 2005), 38.

DECONSTRUCTING ENCOURAGEMENT

It will be worth your while here if we deconstruct encouragement and look at its elements. This way, you'll be able to acquire and use the skill.

First, let's look at the element of unconditional encouragement. Have you ever been in the spectator gallery, or on the receiving end, when someone says, "I know we haven't always got on well, but I just wanted to thank you for your part in this project" or, "I think you performed brilliantly here – no matter what the others say"? Each comment contains encouragement but it is grafted onto a condemnatory criticism. The result is that the melody of encouragement is drowned out by the discord of criticism.

Some time ago, I was providing stress-management training for a group of about 100 specialists in an international telecom business. During the evening session, the managing director of the department delivered his state-of-the-union address over the evening meal. He thanked the staff for a great year and then said, "But I'm going to need 110 percent and more from you next year, okay?" Immediately, his exhausted team lost the benefit from his encouragement surrounding the previous year's performance as it drained away with the realization that more was required. I have seen school principals do the same at the end of a term and team leaders repeat this mistake at annual reviews. True encouragement that inspires real hope will always be unconditional. Otherwise, it gets lost in the noise.

Secondly, if you want to be an effective encourager, you will need to deliver specific and detailed comments. "Well done team," or "Great job everyone," may have the ring of enthusiasm about it, but each individual will have made their own distinctive contributions to the project and deserves to be specifically recognized. They will be much more interested in comments which start with, for example, "I particularly like the way you handled this, or crafted that, or combined these ideas...." In this way, the real work in recognized, the individual is affirmed, and the energy released. True encouragement which inspires real hope will always be specific and detailed.

HUMANS, NOT CAMELS

Thirdly, in order to glean some further insights into encouragement, ask yourself, "How often do I need encouragement and of what should it consist?" If you are a typical racer, it will be clear to you need a regular diet of encouragement.

It's a well known fact that camels can take a drink and, with that, store up resources for long periods of desert drought, living off their supply without needing a fill-up. While it may be true that a little encouragement can go a long way, we humans don't possess camel-like storage capacity in a heated marketplace. You and I need regular sources of encouragement to build up our overall strength and keep us moving forward with a sense of meaning, purpose, and hope.

What is more, your diet will be most nutritious if it is varied. An email, a fax (remember them?), a letter, or a gift, all are capable of feeding the soul. This is why we have awards and prizes, employee recognition programs, incentives, and bonuses. At the heart of the matter is the fact that you need the right words spoken at the right time, spoken in the right way, on a regular basis, from the right people. This is the framework for growth. True encouragement that inspires hope will be regular, consistent, and varied. It therefore involves the discipline of remembering to not only think encouragingly but to act out those thoughts.

When the carpenter responded to the thief with encouragement, the thief knew it was a sincere reply because it was consistent with the way he had seen Jesus work. The reply was not merely a set of words. His language was his life, his reactions, his manner, his style, and lastly his words. But words were only one part of his language.

The lesson here is that the power of hope is released by a large repertoire of encouraging actions. Your working practices can all combine to communicate good news to the person right next to you. The way you handle a team meeting, pay a bill, appoint a staff member, deal with conflict, handle your own stress, and speak your words all form an image of you and what you stand for in the minds of those around you.

LISTEN, LISTEN, LISTEN

As we continue to eavesdrop on this brief encounter between the carpenter and the thief, you can deepen your understanding of the moment by realizing that Jesus of Nazareth, who had every reason to be pre-occupied with his own issues, listens to the person by his side. We can be sure that he really listened because his reply was customized.

To give someone the gift of listening is to give them one of the most expensive gifts you can give. It communicates respect, value, and commitment. Before you listen to your doubts about where I am heading with this, remember that, in this marketplace world, matters such as encouragement, hope, and listening are not just related to the finish line of your race, but directly affect the bottom line of your business. People who work within a climate of encouragement and who are hallmarked by hope will work well, period.

Now, back to the encounter. In this bleak context of dying breaths, the lesson of listening contributes to the concept of hope that we are exploring. Listening is more than just waiting for your turn to speak. Real listening must be focused on the words, background, and character of the speaker. When the thief spoke, Jesus quickly heard his words but also listened to his heart, life story, and journey. Using his listening skills enabled him to tailor his answer to the thief's request. Here are three examples of what I'm talking about: The thief had stolen his rewards – Jesus offered him the gift of a future. This thief had lived with lies – Jesus told him the truth. This thief got what he deserved – Jesus offered him something which he didn't deserve. It certainly would have been captivating to realize the contrast between what this man had experienced throughout his life and what he was experiencing during this interaction in his last laps.

GOOD-NEWS MOMENTS, NERVES, AND WORDS

When you really listen to the person next to you, you are being good news. If you want to communicate with your colleagues, listening will help you learn how to do so. These principles apply to any conversation in which you want to enable someone to get to a better understanding of an issue. They apply if you want to influence someone for good and are certainly relevant if you want to win somebody over to your point of view. Such encounters take place every day in the workplace. You make deals, work with teams, or pair up with an individual to achieve a goal.

Sometimes, people of faith want to introduce a friend or colleague to their faith without having a debate about specific beliefs. You may be party to such a conversation in your marketplace. You might be the person of faith or the one on the receiving end. If you are the latter, it might help you to know that when a colleague is trying to share their faith with you, it is one of the most nerve-wracking of challenges for them. They want to explain to you something which is very important to them without offending you. You may want to try and be encouraging to them, even if you eventually end up agreeing to disagree.

If, on the other hand, you are the one wanting to communicate your faith to a friend at work, then I suggest you listen to them and they will tell you the language to use. This will save a lot of embarrassing elements, irrelevant comments, and awkward moments. To understand what I mean, remember that Jesus spoke to farmers about farming, fishermen about fishing, and shepherds about sheep. So what do we do? We talk about farming, fishing, and sheep! In some marketplaces this may be right, but in the big city where I live there aren't any of these rural professions. There are plenty of teachers, lawyers, accountants, financiers, realtors, and traders of all descriptions. There are engineers, builders, and plumbers. To be good news to anyone, you must learn their language. And to learn their language requires listening.

ON YOUR LEFT OR RIGHT

Here is the advantage of looking at this exchange between Jesus and his neighbor. If you are trying to be good news, encouraging, and hope-inspiring to anyone, it will be much easier to be so to the person right next to you. For one thing, if you are in the same kind of work, you already know their language. Secondly, no one can turn around to you and say, "You don't understand," (my pressures, issues etc.) because you are in the exact same circumstances as they are. Like Jesus, you may be there for a completely different reason, but you are there nonetheless. Good news, encouragement, and hope emerge when you listen and respond. And these elements thrive in a context of companionship, camaraderie, and proximity. Hope that is relevant is powerful, but to be relevant, you must listen.

One time, I was trying to explain the meaning of forgiveness to an IT professional. I used the examples of pressing delete or running a program which turns the numbers all back to zero. I didn't need to say anymore. He filled in the gaps.

I also tried to explain the meaning of some aspect of the life of faith to an accountant. I spoke of God balancing the books and applying generous, undeserved credit to the account. This language made sense to him and he moved on in his understanding. Teachers speak the language of learning; doctors speak the language of healing; and engineers speak the language of precision. For hope and encouragement to be relevant to anyone, it will be best communicated in their own words. This is true of any kind of exchange, whether the content is about business, faith, or any of a million other issues.

FEEL THE POWER

I was out running a few days before writing this chapter – literally running around the roads where I live in an attempt to keep my body in reasonable shape. The circuit I run is quite hilly and challenging, and I occasionally have to slow down or even walk a few paces if I want to make it. On this particular session, I had just started my run and an elderly gentleman was walking towards me. As I passed, he smiled and said, "Well done!" "Thanks," I grunted back through my heavy breathing. That particular day, I completed my run without any problem! His encouragement had given me the hope that energized me to make it through the miles.

WHERE ARE WE HEADING?

The connection between encouragement and hope is illustrated here in that, when the energy of encouragement is transmitted, it feeds your hope that you will make it through. But through to what? I would suggest that you need daily encouragement to give you the hope you need to make it through the hours of your days, the days of your weeks, and the weeks of your working year. You need encouragement and hope around your projects and your projections, your tasks, and your career.

The brief encounter outside Jerusalem illustrates the energy of encouragement connecting with the power of hope. Notice, however, that there was an unusual timeframe surrounding this exchange. The two men were about to finish, not just a day or a week, but their lives. This criminal was in crisis and required urgent, radical responses.

You may be tempted to assume that here your race departs from the race of the thief. Of course, I hope in some ways it does and that you have many more years of a great life ahead of you. Your time left, I sincerely hope, will be much longer than the four to five hours we are examining here. Whatever your time, however, it is limited. You and I do not race like this forever. Here is where you can connect with your stress lessons: To race without an ultimate hope or dream, or to race with false hopes and counterfeit dreams, will both be stressful and disastrous. You need to race, not only with the short-term hope in your soul that will enable you to make it through your weeks and years, but also with a long-term hope that will enable you to make it through your life, and, I dare say, your death.

Death has been described as the "ultimate statistic" – one out of every one of us dies. You run knowing this race will finish. Your breath will run out and your heartbeats will expire. There is a real end-game and you will be done. You will remember the time when this fact of racing hit you or crept into your consciousness and you may not want to think about it too much, especially if you are having a great time. But is it possible that you could run with a type of encouragement in your soul that would energize you with hope, even in the face of the finish?

WHISPERS OF PARADISE

This brings us back to the exchange of words we're examining. Jesus of Nazareth didn't just communicate comforting statements to help the thief die with dignity. The exchange was not merely designed to equip the thief to cope with the next few hours. These were words with a future, containing an ultimate encouragement and a radical hope. These were whispers of paradise.

To understand what happened here, have a look at the short but dramatic journey that the thief took prior to asking for help. As you do, I invite you also to do a quick self-assessment exercise as I describe the drama. This will help you diagnose your own condition relative to the stages of the thief's mental journey. Just keep asking yourself which phase most describes your state and you can then figure out what you want to do with your results.

The records tell us that there was a criminal on each side of the carpenter and both of them mocked him, joining in with the crowd in the initial stages.[3] They hurled insults at him along with everyone else present. To put it mildly, they were both in a cynical and negative phase. Maybe you are, or can remember when you were in such a phase in relation to this Jewish carpenter. Maybe as I write you are struggling to accept that Jesus of Nazareth can affect your real-world race at all.

As time passed, one of the thieves went quiet, distanced himself both from his companion and the crowd, realized his perilous position, and changed his manner altogether. Several things seem to have dawned on him. First, he and his friend were wrong to insult the carpenter. Second, he recognized that while he, as a criminal, deserved to be executed for his wrongdoing, Jesus hadn't done anything wrong and didn't deserve execution. Finally, the thief recognized what was staring him in the face – that he himself was in big trouble.

In a short space of time our thief reflected on his position, the position

---

[3] For the full account, see Luke 23:26-43

of his friends and the crowd, and the position of the carpenter by his side. It was quite a change. He had, to use a Jungian word, "individuated." He had become his own person, taking responsibility for his own actions and realizing their consequences. Pinned-down he may be, but he has definitely moved.

Perhaps you can be sympathetic. You could be experiencing a dawning realization that, if you keep racing the way you are, you may finish healthy, wealthy, wise, or even be judged a success, but it will not be enough. It is reported that someone asked when Rockefeller, reputed to be the world's richest man, died in 1937, "How much did he leave behind?" The reply was, "All of it." This type of thought focuses your mind. You realize that, while you may spend your race acquiring money, power, or property, you can't take that with you after death.

So what is worth racing for? Is there anything I can take with me at the end? These thoughts quickly lead to, "What if this race is not all there is?" "What if I don't slip into oblivion after I finish?"

NOTHING IS WHAT IT SEEMS

At this point, our thief made an apparently ridiculous request. He had observed the carpenter long enough to recognize that this was no ordinary racer. He had seen the "KING" sign above his head and had decided that there was something unique, unusual, and remarkable about everything surrounding his adjacent, accidental companion. So his request is to be remembered, valued, and recognized. It is a request for hope, from one dying man to another. To an outsider, it was a moment of madness. But nothing was what it seemed on this hill. In a complete turnaround of values, the thief invested his hope in a person whose life was ebbing away.

This, of course, is the central Christian proposition. The work which was unfolding on the Roman cross was designed as a perfect model for your work and gives you secrets for your race. But it also is an invitation to invest your hope in a dying man. It is a gentle and generous proposition to listen to the whispers of paradise and let them energize your race with profound encouragement. It will enable you to run with the power of hope strengthening your stride. What is more, if you are already listening to these whispers, it is a challenge to pass the power of hope on to the person right next to you.

THE PARADISE PROPOSITION

So what was the whisper exactly? Ancient Persian kings had their favorite places in their palaces. These were walled gardens full of exquisite greenery, perfumed with flowers, and, being spacious and luxurious, they were reserved for honored and valued guests. The word they used to describe these gardens was *Paradise*.

So what was on offer here? To grasp the meaning, think of your favorite place to be and also think of your favorite people to be with. Now, consider what is the most valuable thing you can give to them. I suggest that it is…yourself. Jesus extended an invitation to the thief to become an honored guest in his own favorite place and share the most valuable gift he can give to him – his companionship. We can legitimately paraphrase the offer by saying, "You. Me. My place. Tonight."

There is something very personal about this whisper of paradise. You can see this thread running throughout the content of the offer. Jesus started by saying, "*I* tell you the truth," and then said, "With *me*." What he was doing is what he always did – he was dispensing himself as the solution, the reply, and the remedy. You will need a little background to capture these ideas because this whisper started with the words, "I tell you the truth," which was Jesus' trademark phrase.

The older Bible versions put it, "Verily, verily," and Jesus is recorded as saying this phrase more than 100 times. The reason for this repetition is that this carpenter understood himself, not just to be speaking the truth, but to be the truth. He didn't propose a way and say, "Follow it." His style was to explain, "I am the way; follow me." This is a critical characteristic to observe.

The reason for hope is a person and his message was deliberately "self-centered." Not self-*ish*, of course, but centered in himself This was the very reason why the Jerusalem characters put him on the cross in the first place. They could not accept that this Nazarene carpenter was who he claimed to be. But this is the basis of hope: Jesus was proposing *himself* as the resolution of all hopes, dreams, and aspirations, the potential rescuer of all racers, and the person who makes the whole race make sense. To this thief, Jesus of Nazareth was communicating himself as the source of hope, as well as the route to a future where paradise meant a walk with Jesus in his own royal garden.

This may be big-picture, long-term thinking, but it quickly connects to sharp-picture, everyday life. This a hope that you can carry in your heart and that will impact the way you work week-by-week. Although we are concerned about working practices, please don't get the impression that this book is about a moral code, an ethical plan, or an abstention from everything you enjoy. This racer of racers brings about an internal revolution in your running that changes everything for the better. Permanently.

And there you have it. This is a whisper to be carried into every waking hour, every working day, every sleepless night, and every passing year. It is an energizing perspective that is on offer, communicated in non-condemnatory, hospitable terms. It is an invitation to race with hope holding you up and spurring you on.

LAST DAY AT THE RACES

Once heard, this whisper will connect with your timeframe. As you will remember, the exact phrase to the thief contained the word, "today." One day, it will be your "today," but hopefully not literally today. There are more secrets to explore, but one day your time will come. And I don't know about you, but as far as I am concerned, "You – me. My place – tonight," sounds like a great way to go.

If you have been running with this whisper in your soul for some time, let me remind you that being a person of encouragement and a promoter of hope is central to your current vocation, whatever your job title. So every working practice – the way you pay your bills, handle your team meetings, deal with your stress, and finish your projects – has the potential to communicate good news, including the way you handle your mistakes.

THE VERY LAST SURPRISE

Before we race on, let's eliminate one final myth that needs to be silenced by this whisper. This thief had no time to better himself or to embark on any type of reformed life. He had no capacity or currency to earn any of the hope he was offered. This is the last surprise. The whisper of hope, of paradise, is a gift. It is freely given to anyone who wants it. There is no currency that can purchase it and no work that can be done to earn it.

The only thing the thief had time to do was to ask to be remembered. It was not his job to figure out how things would play out. The carpenter on the cross next to him was doing that job. In fact, that was why the carpenter was there in the first place, hanging right beside the thief. That's why he could whisper paradise to the person right next to him at work.

LAP THREE:
A BALANCED LIFE –
THE MEANING OF
MOMENTS

Are you doing the right thing right now? Should you be reading my words or doing something else? I would like to think the answer is "yes" to my first question because I'm writing these words to help you figure out the answers to these very questions.

If you have ever been somewhere or with someone when your mind is somewhere else, you know the challenge of trying to respond to competing demands. You will have certainly been on the receiving end of a conversation when you are acutely aware that your counterpart is not paying attention, showing signs of distraction, and appearing disinterested in the face of your riveting monologue.

Even as you read my carefully crafted script, your mind might be floating to business issues, family demands, financial concerns, or even social engagements. It's a racing rat's chronic challenge – chronic in the sense that is recurring and long-term, and chronic in the sense that it has to do with time.

TIME WAITS FOR NO RAT

You race not just against other racers but against the clock. Time waits for no rat and runs at a steady 60 seconds every minute of your entire life. It's hard enough to keep a good relationship with old Father Time under the best of racing conditions, but you can soon find yourself weighed down with guilt if you miss a deadline, a family occasion, or an important opportunity because you were otherwise occupied.

The problem is that, no matter how dedicated you are, you can only be in one place at one time. It is, as someone has observed, "impossible to be elsewhere and otherwise." Even though you may be, for example, at home and thinking about work, you are actually at home – just missing the occasion. You may be at work thinking about a family concern, but you are at work – just not working well. Some of you may even be at church on a Sunday but thinking about next Wednesday's presentation, meeting, or deadline, thus missing the message.

As part of one of my retreat programs, I invite people to draw out a representation of their lives using circles to illustrate all the roles that they play. The picture might include circles labeled to indicate their roles as parent, colleague, friend, neighbor, cousin, manager, and employee, right through to son or daughter. For some incomprehensible reason, the pictures usually contain about 23 roles.

So here are the challenges: How can you run your race and respond appropriately to those 23 or so demands and play your role effectively? How can you allocate your time to each person or group and maintain a sense of sanity? How can you run without guilt or regret, yet keep good relationships with those who matter to you and need your attention? Crucially, how can you make sure that your own well-being is maintained and you actually achieve a life worth living? How can you ensure you will run a race of significance?

One approach, of course, is to not try at all. Many racers do, by default or accident, go for this option. The result is you pursue your own goals and ambitions with a single-minded, high-achieving drive and ignore any issues that conflict with your interests. Paradoxically, some of you will do this in the name of altruism, proclaiming that your dedication to work is merely an expression of your desire to provide for your family. In fact, you will go to any lengths to provide for your family, except providing them with your presence. You will invest in all kinds of opportunities while avoiding the investment of time with those you love. Many an attendant on my retreat programs will draw a picture illustrating the priorities of their lives. Although family or loved ones are at the top of most lists, when asked to allocate indicators of relative amounts of time spent with these people, the picture changes. Work and sleep are soon realized to be the major consumers of time, and loved ones are left to pick up the proverbial crumbs from the timetable.

This is a stressful way to race. Because, built into the tactic is a long-term flaw, a fault line which will appear eventually in your life. Sooner or later, a realization will dawn upon you that you have misallocated your time and energy. Your loved ones have moved on without you and you have lost opportunities that will not come your way again. You may be rich and successful in your work, but a subtle sense of social and relational poverty starts to blight your soul and your last laps become hallmarked with regret.

Some governments and employers are recognizing this dormant disease that could eventually flare up and damage their workforces. Creative schemes are emerging that are designed to make the marketplace more sensitive to the multiple demands that employees face. These include job-sharing arrangements, flexible working hours, childcare facilities, part-time working, parental leave, and career breaks. Many of these approaches make a real difference to the experience of work and enable all workers, and especially parents, to make a better job of living.

LOSING CONTROL?

There are some parts of this problem, however, which resist most attempts at resolution. If you watch baseball, you will see players frantically run from base to base. You may know how they feel as you run from home to work to social life to church to home maintenance and back to work. You are at high risk of feeling as if you are never fully present at any one base, but constantly and nervously looking forward, backward, and sideways.

If you have ever watched tightrope walkers attempt to cross a ravine using a long pole as an aid, you may identify with them in the feeling of fragility and tension as you attempt to walk your perilous path, keep your cool, and avoid falling off into the valley of failure below. Similarly, if you have seen a plate-spinning act, during which the performer places the plates on sticks and attempts to keep them all spinning simultaneously without letting any smash onto the floor, or a juggler throwing increasing numbers of balls into the air, then you will have in these stage acts an image of the internal feelings of panic, concentration, or just plain weariness that accompany your attempt to find this illusive state – the balanced life.

It is when you experience an unguarded moment or close your eyes for a minute and reflect on your life that the baseball player, tightrope walker, plate spinner, Mr. Guilt, or Mrs. Regret speak to your feelings. It is this inner sense of a life out of control, being driven instead of driving, or just trying to keep a show on the road that's so hard to manage. Financial factors can take you hostage leading you to believe that this is how you are forced to race until a quieter day comes.

Whether you have ignored this challenge or are weighed down with its magnitude, I suggest we now go and take another look at the carpenter's race to find some timeless wisdom for this most modern of dilemmas.

It was in the face of this very challenge of finding a sense of balance in the context of competing priorities that Jesus of Nazareth demonstrated a remarkable skill. It was this skill which contributed, in large measure, to his appeal as a person. His approach to handling his own life made him a magnetic character, attracting individuals to him as they sensed something qualitatively different about his manner. In some respects, this can be seen as the secret of his popularity and his enduring ability to attract followers today. It is not the only secret, but it is of great significance.

To uncover it, you will need to take a look at the third sentence he spoke during his 360 minutes of crossing his finish line. I'll quote it for you shortly, but let me first introduce the moment and set the scene.

There was a large crowd of spectators watching the events from a distance. To avert any rescue attempt, a military guard was stationed near the three central figures on crosses.

Your attention however, should be focused on a small group of five devastated onlookers. These were not there as observers; they were supporters and mourners. This group consisted of one man and four women. The man in the group was called John. He was Jesus' best friend and later went on to author the last of the four Gospels, three New Testament letters, and the last book of the Bible. At this point, however, he was watching his best friend struggle with the closing moments of his life.

The four women are important individuals, but pay attention to one among them in particular. Her name was Mary – the mother of Jesus of Nazareth. She had seen her son's entire 33-year race, from remarkable child to unfathomable boy, to educated young man, to carpenter and craftsman, and for the last three years, traveling teacher. She had seen things that astounded her. She heard words that took her breath away. Now she was watching, with heart-wrenching sadness, her invincible son apparently powerless, her supremely articulate son struggling for breath. It is almost impossible to imagine the feelings of John and Mary as they watched this personal nightmare unfold.

Perhaps more than most, they had a hunch that this was no ordinary event. Jesus had explained time after time that this scenario was meant to be and he had constantly explained its meaning. He had laid out for them that this was the work he came to do and how these events were the fulfillment of his life's purpose. Understandably, however, they would have been consumed with grief, and I very much doubt that they were thinking in these terms at this point.

But we must think in these terms, otherwise, we will miss the significance of what happened between these three that day.

THE SECRET OF BALANCE

Not surprisingly, it was John himself who provided us with a record of the incident. Now, let's replay John's words to capture the context of the moment:

"When Jesus saw his mother there, and the disciple who he loved standing nearby, he said to his mother, 'Dear woman, here is your son,' and to the disciple, 'Here is your mother.' From that time on, this disciple took her into his home."[1]

The words took only seconds to say, but the content lasted a lifetime. This brief sentence provides you with a window through which you can look and learn the secret of living a balanced life – not just through corporate policies, but in personal experience that will speak into your chorus of baseball players, plate spinners, and jugglers. To look properly through this window, I suggest you look at the momentous nature of what Jesus was experiencing. As far as he was concerned, this was the most significant task he had ever done. It had, for him, a meaning and purpose of global proportions in that he saw it as the final task of his life's mission to rescue humanity from self-destruction.

Some of you reading this are already totally convinced of these interpretations and consider yourselves to be beneficiaries of this rescue work. Others may be less certain, but if you have read this far you are at least open to exploring these events.

---

[1] The Gospel of John 19:26-27. It may help you to know that John often referred to himself as "The disciple who he loved."

Even if you take the scene at face value, simply acknowledging that it is a man dying in desperate difficulty, what happened next still provides you with a remarkable and astonishing lesson for your life. Either way, this is a monumental moment so demanding, potentially all-consuming, and so distracting that it has the capacity to drown out all awareness of any person or event other than the fact of dealing with one's own death.

But the record shows you another startling surprise, as John informs us that "He saw" his mother and his best friend. What just happened? With every reason to be totally self-absorbed and consumed in his own issues, Jesus is concerned with others. The spectators become the observed ones. The watchers are now watched. The bystanders are now in his sight.

THE POWER OF NOW

To put it another way, Jesus was involved in the momentous, but he was present in the moment. He is engaged in his vocation but concerned about his mother and best friend. That is why people searched him out. He never let the big picture obscure the details; he never ignored the individual as he pursued his goals. When people met him – they *met* him.

John's own account of his friend's story contains interview after interview, encounter after encounter, between Jesus and specific individuals. There are daylight meetings with women who no one valued and night-time meetings with lawyers who wanted advice. There was help for a caterer at a wedding and comfort for grieving sisters at their brother's funeral. And only a few hours before this incident, John had had his feet washed by his friend, and in that moment, nothing else mattered.

Throughout the three years that John had been in his company, he had seen this intense, in-the-moment presence time and time again. Ironically, Mary had seen it too from her perspective of receiving his undivided attention, but also while watching him give this attention to others. Mary had learned, probably the hard way, that her son specialized in focusing on the right person at the right time, even when she didn't want to share him with the world.

The question then arises: How it is possible to develop this art, science, or skill of being fully present in the moment, and at the same time being sure that you are doing the right thing? How is it possible to develop this complex lifestyle of balance in the way he did, while achieving the right goals?

RIGHT THING, RIGHT TIME

Writer John Ortberg defines balance as doing the right thing at the right time.[2] Years before, Saint Augustine spoke about doing the right things at the right time *in the right way for the right reasons*. Both thinkers have identified the nature of balance, but the outcomes will always be a full and rich engagement with the present moment.

Suddenly you are looking at a combination of characteristics. It is one thing to be fully present in the moment, but it is not so useful if you are fully present and absorbed in the inappropriate, doing the wrong thing at the right time. Balance combines presence with rightness. And to do that, we have to look back on the carpenter's previous laps to capture his underlying skills.

---

[2] John Ortberg, *The Life You've Always Wanted* (Zondervan, 1997), 54.

LIFE SKILLS OF BALANCE

Let me give you a simple, personal illustration that may help uncover the first underlying skill that enabled the carpenter to be present in the moment, doing the right thing at the right time.

When I got married, I brought with me an extremely small toolkit with which to carry out any home-maintenance tasks. It consisted entirely of one slightly bent, partially damaged wood-handled screwdriver. With this tool, I scraped paint off walls, lifted carpet from floors, prized nails out of inappropriate places, and using the handle, hammered nails into appropriate places. As you can imagine, the process was somewhat laborious on these projects but the wood-handled screwdriver really came into its own when I used it to screw screws into wood, walls, or wall anchors. This is when it fulfilled the purpose for which it was designed.

SKILL NUMBER ONE: PURPOSE

You and I will need to develop an ever-increasing understanding of the purpose for which we were designed. With that in mind, here is another simple illustration of a profound skill that's essential to your ability to live the balanced life. I once heard of a teenager who, in an argument with her mother, blurted out in a most creative way, "What are you for?"

It's a powerful question because if you have no overall sense of the purpose of your life, how on earth can you attempt to prioritize your time, allocate yourself to any of your roles, or choose how you will spend your energy? If you don't know what really matters to you or what it means to fulfill the purpose for which you were designed, you will have persistent paralysis and confusion when it comes to day-to-day decision making or long-term planning.

If you were to run beside the carpenter with a microphone and ask him for an immediate response to the questions, "Why are you here?" "What is your mission?" Or, "What is your purpose?" you would get instant, thought-out responses. They would be phrases such as, "I didn't come to be served but to serve and to give my life as a ransom for many,"[3] or, "I have come that you may have life,"[4] or again, "I have come to set the prisoners free,"[5] or, "I am the good shepherd who lays down his life for the sheep."[6]

If you feel like a racer who has been taken hostage, drained of life, become trapped, or neglected, these statements will be music to your ears because his purpose is about setting you free, springing you from traps, and nurturing your soul. You may also notice in passing that his statements of life purpose find ultimate expressions in his last hours, when he actually lays down his life.

It may be tempting to stop and examine the content of his statements and enjoy their results for our fulfillment, but our goal here is to simply recognize that they exist. Jesus of Nazareth had a deep sense of personal mission and he expressed it in various mission statements, all of which were complementary. Some focused on being ("I am...") and some focused on doing ("I have come to..."). This then is the first underlying skill: To live in the moment and do the right thing at the right time, you need to know the purpose of your life.

---

[3] Matthew 20:28

[4] John 10:10

[5] Luke 4:18

[6] John 10:11

A LIFE SENTENCE

Companies, organizations, and charities often have their corporate mission statements designed to galvanize people around a common cause and shared goals. What we are examining is a personal mission statement that will release you into your quest for balance.

Before I attempt to give you a small toolkit to help you develop your own mission statement, I must tell you that not everyone thinks this is a wise course of action. Writer and thinker, Os Guinness, is very skeptical. He asks in his book, *The Call*, "Can you state your identity in a single sentence? No more should you necessarily be able to state your calling in a single sentence. At best, you can only specify a part of it...." Again he argues, "Many people use the word 'calling' only for the core of our giftedness. They speak as if we should all be able to specify our callings as a single task expressed in a single sentence. But both people and life are richer than that, and calling is comprehensive, not partial."[7]

After working for many years as a coach for many individuals, I have to say that I disagree with these statements. I quote them because they are well-written from a person I respect enormously. But the issue is not the concept of the single sentence, but the construction and meaning of that sentence. It was not a problem to the most vocationally articulate world changer himself to state his identity and calling in single sentences. The issue is what those sentences mean.

Let me give you an example. If I said to you, "Suzy is my daughter," that would be a true statement of fact and would give you some basic biographical information. For me however, that sentence is teeming with memories of childbirth, games, laughter, tears, schooldays, college

---

[7] Os Guinness, *The Call* (Word, 1998), 51, 52.

degrees, celebrations, teenage chaos, and rollercoaster emotions, to mention just a few. The point is that the sentence is rich beyond imagination *to me*.

One more example may be useful here. Every so often, in fact as infrequently as I can, I book a mobile auto repair man to come and service my vehicle. When he arrives, he says to me, "Hi, I have come to service your car." Now, to me that is a fact and I will pay at the end of the process, but between his words and my payment there is a blank space. I have little or no idea of what he is going to do. For him, with 30 years or so of experience in auto maintenance, that sentence is full of nuts, bolts, oil, spanners, parts, wires, and plugs. It contains a million tasks with names I know not and keeps him occupied for his working life.

My point is that a proper mission statement sets up a dynamic between you and your sentence. It becomes a life sentence, not of confining prison proportions, but characterized by liberation, creativity, and release. Properly crafted, it will grow with you and move with you as you breathe it in and out of your being. Handled correctly, a mission statement can be your means of saying "yes" or "no" to tasks, projects, and people.

There is an amusing incident in John's account of his friend, the carpenter, when a dispute broke out about the religious rite of ceremonial washing, or baptism. As usual, something secondary had been promoted to primary importance and now people were dividing. As this dispute threatened to spread, John recorded for us that, when Jesus learned of this, *he left*.[8] He had not come to get involved in disputes. He was on a mission and would not be deflected. It is the same single-mindedness which drove him to refuse the crowd's desires

---

[8]   John 4:3

to install him as a political, military figure to remove the Romans from authority. That was not his mission any more than getting involved in ceremonial disputes.

MENTAL TOOLS FOR MISSION STATEMENTS

How, then, can you develop your own personal mission statement? Whole books have been written on this subject and consultants have made large sums of money advising clients on these matters. I'm going to suggest some mental tools that are consistent with the carpenter's approach and will help you make some progress. Here we go.

The first tool has to do with taste. I suggest you ask yourself what you love doing, long to do, and find great pleasure in having achieved. This is not a self-centered quest but a diagnostic question that gives you a clue to your design and how that will express itself in your mission. There is a noble but misguided notion that has spread through our culture; it associates calling with doing something painful, sacrificial, outside of your comfort zone, and so selfless as to be in a different category to your desires. If you are already quite comfortable with the idea that your personal mission and vocation should also be deeply satisfying and pleasurable, then you need no further convincing. If you retain a certain uneasiness about these ideas, then maybe this is worth a little reflection.

It is a simple fact of life that, if you want to achieve or be anything of significance, the drive and energy for that achievement will originate from within your inherent design. Your desires, gifts, and strengths will be the volcano out of which your mission will explode.

You can see this in so many environments if you are prepared to look. Consider how employers appoint employees. They look for past achievements, personal ambitions, qualifications, and talents. They are constantly asking, "What does this person do well, what do they want to achieve, what have they done that tells me what they are about, and, by implication, what do they enjoy doing?" In other words, how is this person wired, designed, or configured? If you go for an interview, these are the aspects of yourself you must demonstrate to show your prospective employers how you fit with the job they are advertising. The process is most powerful when there is a fit between the person you were designed to be and the job that needs to be done.

Let me quote you some words from Frederick Buechner:

Vocation comes from the Latin Vocare, *to call, and means the work a person is called to by God. There are all different kinds of voices calling you to all different kinds of work, and the problem is to find out which is the voice of God rather than of Society, say, or the Superego, or Self-Interest.*

By and large a good rule for finding out is this: The kind of work God usually calls you to is the kind of work (a) that you need most to do and (b) that the world most needs to have done. If you really get a kick out of your work, you've presumably met requirement (a), but if your work is writing cigarette ads, the chances are you've missed requirement (b). On the other hand, if your work is being a doctor in a leper colony, you have probably met requirement (b), but if most of the time you're bored and depressed by it, the chances are you have not only bypassed (a), but probably aren't helping your patients much either.

Neither the hair shirt not the soft berth will do. The place God calls you to is the place where your deep gladness and the world's deep hunger meet.[9]

---

9 Frederick Buechner, *Wishful Thinking: A Seeker's ABC* (Mowbray 1994), 118.

As you can see, he finishes his reflection with a combination. Calling, as he defines it, is a meeting place between "your deep gladness and the world's deep hunger." Stress managers such as myself often speak of a person-environment fit. This is the same idea but also contains the notion of a bad fit or mismatch where stress could increase. When you're doing something that doesn't fit with who you are you don't enjoy it, you underperform and miss out on your potential. On a sports field, this would be called "playing out of position." What we are looking at is the importance of being in position, finding a fit, and letting your deep gladness connect with the world's deep hunger.

This is an important factor for wise thinking about your mission. Keep asking yourself "What am I good at?" "What are my strengths?" "How am I wired?" This way, you will be starting your journey towards your mission statement.

Don't get me wrong; I am not saying that there is no sacrifice, struggle, or pain in finding and fulfilling your mission. What I am saying is that, as you clarify the content of your deep gladness, design, and therefore mission, you will be prepared to go through all kinds of sacrifices, struggles, and pains to discharge it.

That's what was happening on this desolate Jerusalem hill. Here was a man who had figured out the gladness, joy, and rewards related to his life's purpose, and was spending himself to fulfill it. He is not enjoying these six hours; he is enduring them because he knows that there is a reward to follow – or, to be more specific, billions of followers will be his reward and they will reap the benefits of his sacrifices. The world hungers for rescue and for meaning. And being connected with the carpenter's gladness is the very definition of a meaningful life's race. It's expensive, but it's priceless.

Another mental instrument for you to use in developing your own sense of mission is to ask yourself what you can do that no one else can. This takes you in the direction of responsibility and relates to your individual giftedness. No-one else on this planet can be father to my daughter. There are numerous good male friends that I have who can be great role models and even friends to her, but they can't be her dad – period.

Finding your sense of mission will include not only your unique design but also your unique position. No-one else can stand in your shoes for certain tasks because there are some things you simply cannot delegate or outsource – they are yours alone. This will need to be factored into your life's mission statement, and we will look at aspects of this when we look at the next secret regarding struggle and integrity. Although we are looking at seven sentences separately, you may be realizing that you will need to draw on all the wisdom of the carpenter to develop your sense of mission. For now, it will be rewarding to recognize that he made sure he discharged the duties which he and he alone could do and this sharpened his mission focus.

On your journey of discovery, don't be afraid to live with hanging, unanswered, or half-answered questions. If you are going to write a sentence that starts with, "The purpose of my life is…," you need to think about your design, gladness, gifts, talents, wiring, and duties, but you will also find yourself wrestling with a range of questions. This is not a bad place to be because questions are rich mental nutrients that will nourish your thinking and fill out your ability to clarify. They contain slow-acting, long-lasting ingredients. They work their way into your life and find the un-repaired, derelict areas and, little by little, restore your soul. So keep living with them, in them, and on them as your sense of mission develops and helps you to live in the present and do the right thing.

SKILL NUMBER TWO: HANDLING DAYS

So how else can you develop this balanced life? I suggest you now take a look at that most common of experiences that occurs seven times a week and 365 times each year of your race. I'm referring, of course, to the day.

Living a balanced life is linked to your ability to handle a day. This is not as straightforward as it may seem because we humans have the ability to play mental tricks on ourselves and lose our balance in this most testing of races. So here are a few racing tips from the carpenter for you to equip yourself to make it through the day.

In one of the most profound expressions of wisdom that we now call the Sermon on the Mount, Jesus of Nazareth advised us all with, "Do not worry about tomorrow."[10] It's a fantastic bit of advice because spending your mental energy on days that have not yet arrived will rob you of the ability to live in the day that has. Worry has extraordinary skill in the art of distracting your attention and is therefore is one of the most sophisticated stealers of the peace of the present. Before you realize it, worry walks away with the value of enjoying the here and now.

Like stress, worry is better handled when you understand its character. For this reason, we should acquaint ourselves with this thief and develop a range of strategies to defend ourselves against its invasion. To do that, you need to remember that worry is nearly always future-focused. This is why the Sermon on the Mount contains the advice, "Do not worry about tomorrow."

You have the ability to imagine an array of disastrous futures. Let your

---

[10] Matthew 6:34

mind wander and you can conjure up scenarios of plane crashes, market collapses, embarrassing meetings, inadequate budgets, ill health, mistakes, and a million awful outcomes. Without leaving even your room, you can invent countless disturbing dramas in which you fall, others fail or the whole world implodes. In fact, you don't even need to leave the comfort of your own head. We humans, with our big brains, are experts at this ingenious mind game. The problem with this game is that you never win.

In order to capture this thief and restrain its power, you must figure out and use alternative mental strategies to make it through the day. The first one of these strategies arises directly out of the carpenter's advice: Be determined to deal with days one at a time. Have you noticed that this is how they arrive anyway? Of course, in a strange but common practice, we often attempt to deal with them as groups instead of individuals.

I once was giving a talk on this subject and a lady came up to me afterwards and said that the idea of taking one day at a time had been of immense help to her because she had just learned that she was pregnant. Apparently, her previous pregnancy had been extremely difficult and the thought of nine months of struggle filled her with dread. "But," she said, "I think I can deal with one day". She had decided to take the next 270 days one at a time, in manageable steps, and leave the future where it belonged. I had been giving my talk in relation to work and worry, but this wise woman had taken the principle and applied it to her own situation recognizing this significant alternative to worry.

In case you have been racing ahead or lagging behind, let me remind you that we are assembling a mental toolkit to assist you on your quest to live in the present moment and do the right thing at the right time. We are not inventing these tools, but we're deliberately opening up the carpenter's tool box and seeing how the master craftsman fashioned a balanced life. We have looked at personal mission as it relates to your whole life. We are now looking at handling each and every day well and we are focusing on dealing with the thief of time called worry. We have identified an initial strategy to take one day at a time and I now suggest you consider how to start and finish a day.

TOP AND TAIL

You may remember our angry and stressed-out swordsman who we met on lap one – the one who cut off a servant's ear. His name was Peter and he is now widely accepted as the brains behind the book we know as the Gospel of Mark. It's a fast moving book, full of action, and short on reflection. The calm life of the contemplative was not for Peter and Mark; they were connected to the fishing industry, and storms were more their style. All the more remarkable, then, that you find two small incidents recorded that give you further insight into the way the carpenter handled his days and managed to live a balanced life fully present in each moment.

Mark's gospel records for us that, "Very early in the morning, while it was still dark, Jesus got up, left the house, and went off to a solitary place where he prayed."[11]

I don't know about you, but I'm not really a morning person. I prefer to approach mornings from the end of the previous day rather than at the sunrise of the current one. I often stay up into the small hours just to make sure I have not missed anything of interest. With the passing of time, I am discovering that mornings are not such a bad idea and I get some of my best writing done during them.

---

[11] Mark 1:35

The point is that, whatever your biorhythmic physiology, whether you are a morning or an evening person, or a shift worker, there is a point where your day begins. The carpenter's habit was to begin the day by communicating with his Father. Here we have again a "Father" prayer. This time, however, there may have been a particular emphasis. We don't know the content of this prayer, but in that famous Sermon on the Mount we have a model prayer which contains a specific reference to a daily activity. You will have almost certainly prayed it yourself numerous times. The daily part is, "Give us today our daily bread."[12]

In western culture, we can sometimes miss the meaning behind this request. While I was in Africa, I met people who, each day, needed to engage in work that would enable them to eat that day. For them, "Give us today our daily bread," was a literal request for regular resources.

Behind this way of praying is a way of thinking and racing. It recognizes that each day is a gift from the creator and that each day contains its own challenges and needs. While it encourages an attitude of thankfulness for the day, it also evokes the sense of dependency by encouraging you to ask your Maker to make your day. In so doing, you develop a heart condition of regular trust in the ultimate supplier of your needs. The request can be phrased, "Give me today what I need for today." When you put it like that, you may be able to see how this can equip you to take one day at a time. It's another lock on the door to keep out the thief of worry.

This attitude of trust that, on the very day you need them, resources will be there (thankfully not too late, but irritatingly, from your point of view, never too early) can enable you to consider how much your life is driven by a desire to have more than you need. Many an

---

[12] Matthew 6:11

unbalanced life is lived that way because greed has replaced need, and luxury has misplaced necessity. The result is that you have created a lifestyle that itself has become a hungry monster snarling at you and forcing you to spend yourself just to feed its voracious appetite.

An 18th-century physician and educator once observed, "Fortunate indeed is the man who takes the right measure of himself and holds a just balance between what he can acquire and what he can use."[13] Think for a minute how your life would look if you built it around believing that, on each and every individual day, the mental, physical, emotional, and spiritual resources necessary for that day would be there on a daily basis. Tomorrow's resources will be there tomorrow and the next day's resources will be there the day after. Your job is to manage the 1,440 minutes you get every 24 hours, and handle those daily resources wisely.

Surely this would focus your mind more on the present and enable you to discover another dimension to the carpenter's secret of living a balanced life. Starting the day with this dependent attitude is a tool straight out of the carpenter's toolbox.

Starting the day is one thing, finishing is another. For most of you, it is not really meaningful for you to say that your work is done or your job is finished. Have a look at this sentence:

Thereisalwayssomefurthertaskprojectorchallengearoundthecorner.

It is very difficult to read a sentence with no punctuation or spaces. In the same way, it is very difficult to live a life with no commas, pauses or full stops. In your work, it is quite likely that you must

---

13 http://en.thinkexist.com/quotation/fortunate_indeed-is_the_man_who_takes_
exactly_the/11729.html

decide where to put the pauses, take the breaths, or stop altogether. Although projects may finish, there is always something else to do. One of the curses of modern marketplace culture is the habit of working long hours. Many of us think that we are working well when we have really gone past the sell-by date of the day. Stress research has repeatedly shown that going past optimum thresholds, such as 48 hours in a working week, will result in less work per hour for each overtime hour worked. Beyond a certain point, productivity and effectiveness decrease.

The question is, therefore, do you know how to stop? Do you know when your day is over and it's time to go home? When is it time to put down the tools or switch off the PC? If you love your work, and I hope you do, this may be an even bigger challenge for you. If you work from home, as millions do, finishing the day may mean walking from one room to another, and the temptation to walk back later will be similar to that experienced by others as they arrive through the door with briefcase, notebook, or cell phone at the ready.

The fact is, if you don't know how or when to stop your working day, you will greatly diminish your ability to be present where you are. Because where you are will always be distorted by where you work. The challenge is not to learn to despise your work, but to celebrate it when you are doing it, being fully present as you do so, then transition healthily to other present moments that are alternative, restful, or qualitatively different. This challenge is also the invitation to do other things during your day so that nothing dominates to the detriment of everything or everyone else (including you).

Peter and Mark record a second moment that happened at the beginning of the week, which we audited in our stress audit, but it also happened at the end of the day: "Jesus entered Jerusalem and went into the temple. He looked around at everything but since it was already late, he went out to Bethany with the twelve."[14]

It's an almost insignificant piece of historical information. Peter would have been looking over Jesus' shoulder as he looked around the temple, and when they left, they would have almost certainly gone to Mark's house for the meal. So both men record the incident for you. Contained in it, however, is more than a piece of biographical information. Here you can see the carpenter showing his team that the day is finished and the work is done. They had had a remarkable day, but it is now over. It is time to stop.

This is all the more startling because, the very next day, the carpenter-turned-rebel would walk into the temple with a whip and sign his own death sentence with each lash. This was taking place the day before he cleared out the market traders and started his classic confrontation with the powers that be. But this day was over.

It is a powerful discipline and can be captured when you decide that you will find the end point of your working day. For some of you, it will mean symbolically closing a door in your home. For others, it will mean choosing a finish time which you honor for yourself and your loved ones. For still others, it may involve telling your team that they must stop for the day and go home.

If you are in a position of influence, you may have been operating a regime that forces staff to sacrifice their lives on the altar of bad working practices, based on too few personnel. Job specifications and organizational culture may need to be examined to see if the workloads are human-sized. One thing we will all need to keep in mind is that knowing when to stop did not stop the carpenter from changing the world – quite the opposite, in fact. It will not stop you from achieving

---

[14] Mark 11:11

your goals either. This brings us to another part of the toolkit – knowing the nature of success.

SKILL NUMBER THREE: BEING CLEAR ABOUT SUCCESS

I have not met anyone who did not want to be a success. I have met plenty of people who have had completely different ideas about the nature of success, but however unusual or non-conformist they are, they all want to measure up to their own scales. This thinking does beg a very important question: What is success? Without a satisfactory answer to this question it will be impossible to do the right thing at the right time or to be fully present in the moment. If you have no idea of what you are trying to achieve, how can you spend your energy achieving it?

We have already started down the road to answering this question because we can now say that success can be linked to fulfilling your personal mission, learning to handle days well, and figuring out what right things are to be done. Asking this specific question will open up a few other windows for you and bring some light onto your balancing act.

Someone once observed that, for most of his life, he had been climbing a ladder only to discover it was leaning against the wrong wall. I want to suggest to you that, if you can gather together the thinking of this chapter so far, you will be formulating your definition of success. I would further suggest that you consider one of the carpenter's famous questions that will connect with our anonymous ladder climber's lament.

The question is, "What good is it for you to gain the whole world, yet forfeit your soul?"[15]

---

[15] Mark 8:36

This question proposes that gaining the world but losing your soul is a poor deal. Try looking at the question this way. What good is it if you have extreme success in one area of your life (gain the whole world) at the expense of all the other areas of your life(your soul)? What good is it if you are brilliant at business but your children never see you? What good is it if you are a great friend to your friends but waste your unique talents? What good is it if you make a fortune but destroy your relationships?

If you come across this dying carpenter on a bleak hill, the view you get doesn't look like success. But here is a man fulfilling his life's purpose, doing the right thing at the right time, and being fully present in the moment. He has seen past the pain to paradise and is absolutely certain of his destiny. Is this not a picture of success? He has got the big picture in view and all his energy is expended on the essentials. These essentials include John and Mary, his friend and mother, who he sees as they watch him die. And he thinks of their future even as he takes his last breaths.

So success is multi-layered, not monolithic. Success is to live in rich, purpose-filled moments containing combinations of various achievements. We are not talking about the emptying of minds but a fulfillment of dreams on a daily basis, utilizing an array of tools to construct these complex moments in a continual flow.

SKILL NUMBER FOUR: THE NOBLE ART OF PLANNING

Before you get too carried away, there are a couple more useful tools to consider that will help you maintain your balance. In the middle of all this talk about living in the present, taking one day at a time and not worrying about tomorrow, you must also remember the skill of planning.

This carpenter was a master planner. If you are prepared to look at his life as a whole, you will see that he prepared himself by learning languages, acquiring a trade, running a business, living in a family, and observing his world.

You cannot achieve what he did in the last three years of his life without meticulous and dedicated planning. He didn't suddenly develop the ability to handle trick questions – he learned to deal with difficult customers in his business. He didn't spontaneously acquire the art of storytelling – he had been listening and watching all his life as he grew up in a real family. It's a tribute to his own human father that he spoke so easily of the Father prayers. He was a planner through and through. If you look at his 36 months of public work, you can see that he had a geographical plan, covering the north and south of the country, as well as taking various strategic trips as they fit with his people plan. His people plan included gathering his team and training them, going out of his way to meet specific individuals, and making sure he ended up dealing with the decision makers. He had a consistent, clear, and repeated message strategy designed to lay out his manifesto for the world to see.

If you are willing to look at the whole Bible narrative, you will find that there are 60 major predictions about his life, written before he was born, which found their resolution in his plans. Of these, 29 connected with this very day we are examining.

Here was a man who knew exactly what he was doing. You don't get half the world to follow you, 2,000 years after you're gone, by accident. He planned his race for maximum impact, including planning to arrive at this moment of execution. He could have pulled out, he could have lead a revolution, as the crowd craved, or he could have just run away, but he planned to keep his appointment.

There is a massive difference between planning and worrying.

Worrying imagines a disastrous future and allows the worrier to be disturbed with panic and dread. Planning examines future possibilities and prepares for them while defining the preferred option and putting energy into achieving it. Worrying is associated with anxiety, planning dissolves anxiety and washes the clutter out of your mind. There is nothing grubby or mundane about planning. It is a noble art. And with it, you can paint a picture of your future instead of shrinking back in horror at its appearance.

SKILL NUMBER FIVE: CREATIVE DELEGATION

Another functional tool worth gathering from this moment is that of delegation. Many a moment has been damaged by a racer who is doing something that would be done better by someone else. You may already be an expert in this skill, but most racers are not. There is a saying that, if you want a job done properly, you have to do it yourself. It's nonsense. If you want a job done properly, you have to find the most skillful person to do it. That's the challenge and the core meaning of "properly." How much energy do you waste on tasks that are outside of your skill set or responsibility? Delegation is not a luxury; it is a recognition of legitimate limits and a celebration of the variety of talents in the human race. Just as you will find your mission by acknowledging what you love doing, so you will learn to delegate by passing on to others those tasks that they love doing and will do much better than you.

I can do administration, but I'm not great at it and I don't love it. I watch with unbridled delight someone who loves administration taking the tasks out of my in-box. While you think about delegation, you may discover that there are some things you are doing that actually don't need to be done at all. Many teams have audited their procedures and discovered that certain reports are not being read by anyone, or that some pieces of work produce no results worth chasing. These

109

items can be delegated to the shredder.

In the moments approaching his death, Jesus of Nazareth delegated the responsibility of caring for his mother to his best friend and the care of his best friend to his mother. To do this, he used the simple phrase, "Woman, here is your son. ...Son, here is your mother."[16]

Tradition tells us that John took Mary into his home and she moved with him to his new post in Ephesus. If that is the case, you can be sure that Mary's wisdom and insight is wrapped up carefully in John's writings and has greatly enriched our understanding of the carpenter's race.

SKILL NUMBER SIX: THE MEANING OF IMPORTANT

You will remember when I set the scene for you that there were five people in this small group which contained John and Mary. The other three were Mary's sister and two other women, both of whom were also called Mary. These other three women were faithful and loyal supporters who mattered to Jesus very much. But in this moment they were not as important to him as Mary and John, the two we are considering. Here is a strange but vital skill to adopt in finding your balance. Not everyone can be treated with equal importance, given equal time and energy out of your human resources. You cannot be everyone's friend, supporter, or solution. To maintain balance, you must choose to focus on a specific individual or group of individuals and that choice will sometimes be painful.

Not long after I founded the organization for which I work, I took my wife and daughter away for a much-needed break. As we were walking

---

[16] John 19:26-27

together on a windswept beach on the south coast of England, I asked my daughter what she thought of my new work. Her 12-year-old reply made me stop in the sand: "It's good dad, but the family doesn't see so much of you anymore." This was a shock to me, like a sharp punch in the pit of my stomach. I had always made a point of spending quantities and qualities of time with my family, not out of duty but out of delight. I had given my daughter regular and protected times in my diary, as well as my general ongoing presence of a father. As I asked her to clarify what she meant, it turned out that one of her main concerns was for my tiredness as I started the new work while simultaneously earning a master's degree in stress management and attempting to figure out how to answer new work-related questions.

This brief reality check was enough of an alarm bell to help me reflect on the questions, "Who are the most important people in my life," and, "How am I going to make sure that they know it and never forget it?" The alarm bell provoked me to make several practical changes immediately in our family life, and I will use them as suggestions for you to consider in your own race. Of course, they were in the context of the "married-with-child" model in which I was living, but I recognize that many readers and racers live in very different dynamics.

SKILL NUMBER SEVEN: FINDING YOUR MODEL

The first practical change I made in my life was that I created a space. By purchasing a small table, chairs, and a simple sound system, we made a space in our kitchen that we reserved especially for family meals. Instead of inviting the TV to dine with us, we ate together in the evening on a daily basis and caught up with each other. A large percentage of families never do this and then wonder why they lose touch. Once a week, we had a Sunday lunch followed by a short prayer and catch-up time. We are not the most spiritual family in the world, but by reviewing the week, previewing the coming week, and having a short reading and prayer, we learned to talk of deeper things in the context of regular life. Symbolically, we would light candles at the beginning of a meal and the meal would not finish until the candle was blown out. The reason for this somewhat quaint and ritualistic behavior was that, while the candle was lit, that was our precious time to be together. No cell phone, fax, land-line, or doorbell would be answered. This time was therefore protected by agreement.

These occasions were so much fun that, over the years, our daughter felt free to bring friends into the meals. And as she became a medical student, to my utter amazement, even other students turned up as guests. Let's not be naïve here. There were times when our daughter found this a pressure when, for example, she needed to get some school work done or wanted to talk with friends. Sometimes we knew we were making life harder for ourselves in the middle of a busy schedule. Nevertheless, I suggest that you learn to protect times with those you love, whether family or friends, and keep them safe from a million and one interruptions.

There are several other aspects to this protection strategy. We learned to use our diaries together. First, this meant just coordinating who was doing what and when – not too hard with a 12-year-old, but as time went by, we were trying to get slots in her busy schedule. On another level, I made dates with my daughter – specific, special times when I was hers and no one else's. At least once a week, she knew that this was her special time and that no one, not even a paying client, was more important.

Not only is it good to protect times but also seasons. For me, Christmas day or Easter Sunday are great celebrations but can come and go so quickly. We learned to wrap Christmas in Advent and Easter in Lent so that we reflected for four weeks or 40 days on the meaning of the season.

The principle is worth capturing, whatever model of life you are living. Schedule time with those you love and don't give the message to them that appointments are always tentative and negotiable. Let them know that you will actually be there.

During times when you are not there, use whatever technology you can to keep in touch. A friend of mine was away a lot on business and his daughter was not a great phone person but loved writing. His solution was to set up an e-mail relationship with her as he traveled. It was not a substitute for his presence, but a massive improvement during his absence.

You should also consider how you can help someone else balance their lives. This may mean babysitting for them or watching their kids while they go on a retreat, or simply house-sitting with the dog.

Balance looks different during life's phases and a person in their 20s may need to go at top speed for some time and maintain their balance while working long hours at a single task. On the other hand, a person in their 50s may be much more involved in a variety of things and need to skip from one set of tasks and relationships to another set. Here, the skill is to talk to others about your own experiences and look at the seasons of your own life. For some of you, the biggest step at the moment might involve just turning off the TV and buying a candle.

SKILL NUMBER EIGHT: ASK A BIG QUESTION

There is one other question for you consider asking in order to learn to live in the present moment and keep doing the right thing. It is a question that I doubt you will ever be able to answer fully, but the mere asking of it will provoke your mind and strengthen your racing style. The question is, "Why am I alive today?"

I'm suggesting in this question that you at least explore what it is about today's world that presents you with unique opportunities to live a fulfilling life. What is the deep hunger out there in the world today that may be different to other generations? For me, a partial answer lies in the fact that I write a weekly e-mail that goes to several thousand racers to help them make it through their working life. Even 20 years ago this technology did not exist. It is not the reason I was born but it is part of my gladness. Give it a thought.

Also remember this: When you get to the end of your race and dribble is coming out of the side of your aging mouth, it will not be your fast-paced team members who show up to wipe it away – it will be someone you loved and who loved you. I advise you to see them, not just at the finish line but intentionally notice them on a daily basis. Because one day, it will be their turn to notice you.

LAP FOUR:
STRUGGLE AND INTEGRITY –
THE GOD-FORSAKEN PATH?

You may not have heard of Christoph Meili. He and his family are reputed to be the only Swiss nationals in history ever to have been granted political asylum in the United States. On January 8, 1997, Christoph decided to remove some files from his place of employment and take them to his home. At the time, Meili was working as a night guard at the Union Bank of Switzerland (UBS) and his actions opened him up to the accusation of violating his nation's strict laws of banking secrecy, an offense that is always prosecuted in Switzerland.

The facts that transformed his action from petty theft to courageous behavior relate to the contents of the files he removed. Christoph had stumbled upon information that indicated that officials at UBS were destroying credit balance documents of deceased Jewish clients. The whereabouts of the rightful heirs to this credit were unknown, but the document destruction was also a serious violation of Swiss law. In destroying these records, the bank may have been clearing the way for itself to appropriate the funds and avoid any further work in locating the heirs.

Christoph Meili handed over his evidence to a local Jewish organization, which in turn passed them on to the police and the press, which duly published his story.

You will almost certainly have heard of Erin Brockovich-Ellis who, four years prior to Christoph's action, as a legal clerk with no formal law school education, helped construct a case against Pacific Gas and Electric that resulted in a $330 million settlement relating to drinking water contamination. Her story was later made into the Hollywood movie *Erin Brockovich*, starring Julia Roberts.

These two characters join an illustrious hall of fame, or maybe of infamy. It includes names such as William Wilberforce, who battled for 20 years to get the British parliament to enact laws abolishing the transatlantic slave trade. It also includes Lord Shaftesbury, who worked for 14 years to enact legislation that reduced the typical working day to 10 hours. And it of course includes people like Martin Luther King, Jr., who worked ceaselessly for a just society for all races prior to his assassination in 1968. We could go on – Florence Nightingale, Abraham Lincoln, Rosa Parks, Mother Teresa....

What these individuals have in common is that they stood for what was right, battled for their beliefs, and persisted in the pursuit of their goals. What they also shared in common is that their actions were almost always at great personal cost to themselves and, even though many others may have joined their causes, supported, or even funded them, they all knew what it meant to experience being alone.

In the end, the decisions these people made led to an inevitable pathway wide enough only for one. It is a strange phenomenon experienced by millions over the centuries but it is not shared because it contains, written in its DNA, the feature of aloneness.

G.K. Chesterton observed that "right is right, even if nobody does it. And wrong is wrong, even if everybody is wrong about it."[1] In contrast, Oscar Wilde observed that the easiest way to deal with temptation is to give into it.[2] You may not find yourself facing an issue like the trans-Atlantic slave trade or massive corporate corruption, but every day you are faced with choices to do the right thing, avoid the wrong, and not give into temptation. In the same way that the endless repetition of brief muscular exercises builds up your strength, so continual practice of integrity prepares you, not only for the next small honorable choice, but for the potential life-changing moment when you realize you must make your stand.

---

[1]   G.K Chesterton *All Things Considered* (Methuen 1919), 199.

[2]   Henry Russell *The Sayings of Oscar Wilde* (Duckworth 1997), 48. Quoting *The Picture of Dorian Gray* chapter 2

The hall of fame we visited earlier may be populated with spectacular examples of extraordinary courage, but it also includes regular people who realized the significance of their positions and the privileged information to which they were party.

Make no mistake about it; there is no automatic, "Thank you" at the end of such processes. In a survey carried out in the U.S. and Britain, it was discovered that 80 percent of whistleblowers interviewed lost their jobs after telling their employer of a fraud to which they were not a party.[3]

If you decide to uncover the darkness, there is a high risk that you will be plunged into the darkness and sucked into the storm of unpleasant, unintended consequences that can take you to the very limits of your ability to cope. Stripped of support, short of cash, and low on friends, you can find yourself in dire straits within a matter of months of your original decision.

THE AGENDA UNFOLDS

Let's broaden our focus a little. This lap is not just about integrity; it's also about struggle. Although the two often go hand in hand, there are some struggles that have a life of their own. It seems to be a principle of life that anyone who has ever achieved anything of significance has faced their own struggles, walked in the darkness, and danced with despair. Even the most optimistic, easy going, carefree racers bleed when they are cut and hurt when they fall.

So our agenda now has four major items on it: struggle, integrity, taking a stand, and being alone. This aspect of the race may be uphill,

---

[3] *The Observer* newspaper, July 8, 2001.

but the view from the top will be worth it. So let me invite you back to the hill outside Jerusalem to eavesdrop on more words from the carpenter-turned-teacher as he faces his sternest test yet.

THE VIEW FROM THE HILL

It's getting dark. We are not talking about the slow dimming of the day as sunset gently gives way to twilight and the pleasant warmth of the evening brings some respite from the heat of the day. This is an aggressive, bleak, and eerie darkness in which nothing is clear and everything is full of foreboding emotions. After a period of silence, a voice pierces the darkness with a disturbing question:

"My God, my God, why have you forsaken me?"[4]

It is the fourth sentence spoken by Jesus of Nazareth as his time comes to a close, and it is not a comfortable phrase to hear. It echoes down through the centuries into all the souls of those who have also cried out in frustration at the awfulness of their struggles. It contains our entire agenda, and more, because it is about integrity and exposing the darkness. And without doubt, this is a phrase of struggle and indescribable isolation. He is alone with himself in this moment, and his work of works has reached the peak of its intensity. This is a window into his work through which we will look carefully because what you see is quite hard to bear and definitely demanding. But you must look if you want wisdom to apply in the dark moments as well as the light. You will need to go to the brink in order to find your way home.

---

[4]   Matthew 27:46 (see also Mark 15:33)

VISITING THE WORST SPACES

As a stress specialist, I sometimes invite individuals to imagine what the worst possible outcome could be in their current circumstances. When they articulate that scenario, we then discuss it and construct a strategy or contingency plan about how it could be faced should that worst outcome materialize. The value of this approach is that it takes the individual to a place so extreme that finding a way to cope there would give them the best survival skills. Additionally, because in real life the worst possible scenario almost never happens, these same extreme survival skills will be more than adequate to deal with the actual outcomes. You can try this exercise right now by asking these two questions:

What is the worst possible thing that could happen here?

If that happened, how would I deal with it?

You can apply these questions to your own individual circumstances and use them as a way of helping yourself engage with the challenge. You can also learn from other people's darkest hours and gather the lessons for yourself by benefiting from the wisdom and experience of others.

This is what you are doing if you look through that window of words – that cry of, "Why have you forsaken me?" that echoed through the darkness You will be able to visit the time that was the worst of all possible moments for Jesus of Nazareth and see how he dealt with it. There are powerful advantages of this approach. As you visit his hardest hour, you can learn about extremes and acquire survival skills that you can bring back into your own race. You can watch him maintain his integrity, even though the struggle and the aloneness are horrendous, so that, when you turn away, the image of his behavior will etch itself into your mind.

Please don't expect what follows to fit into a neatly arranged kit or well-ordered list. The skills I am talking about here tumble out of the darkness and scatter onto the ground. They are designed for difficult and desperate times, and you may find that you will reach out and grasp one life-saving skill while ignoring the others. They are not a pleasant jigsaw puzzle but an emergency supply to be called upon according to your injuries, needs, or crises. So let's start with the skill we'll label "Question."

THE POWER OF QUESTIONS

To gather your skills, first consider the fact that this fourth sentence from the Jerusalem hill is a question. If you observe Jesus' communication style, you will discover that he used questions regularly and for specific reasons. He asked some would-be followers, "What do you want?" He slipped questions like, "Why do you worry?" and "What do you think?" into his teaching. To those who were trying to make up their minds, he asked, "Who do you say that I am?"

Although genuine, his questions were almost always asked for the benefit of the hearer. You can be sure that when he says, "My God, my God, why have you forsaken me?" he not only wants us to hear the question but to engage with it, reflect on it, and explore its meaning. He wants us to come up with some possible answers so that we can learn from this darkness how to race on.

But before we race past the question in search for answers, we need to pause and notice the simple fact that he indeed used a question to make his point. If you research the history of whistle-blowing and the lives of those who took their stands, you will find a catalogue of techniques that they used to broadcast their concerns. Petitions, protests, and dramatic gestures all stand out in the catalogue. Some have observed, however, that one of the most powerful and effective tools that can

122

open up the issues is the asking of provocative questions.

To ask, "Why is this happening?" "What is going on here?" "How did we let this come about?" "Do we really think this is wise?" is to invite people to consider what role they are playing in the episode. Posing the pertinent question can challenge the corporate mentality or group-think, stir consciences, or even create a healthy unease and fear of the possible consequences. How many scandalous stories reach the press containing, somewhere in the text, the comment, "Nobody questioned what was really going on"? We are not talking exclusively about massive issues here. It might be a simple stance on a small but significant point of principle.

Not long ago, I spoke with a young man who relayed to me some comments he had made to prospective employers in a job interview. He had told them that he wouldn't lie for them and he wouldn't lie to them. In that single sentence, he had made his integrity clear. Work environments often include the practice of telling someone on the phone that your colleague is not in the office when he is, in fact, sitting right next to you. There's also the all-too-common practice of telling a customer a product has certain features that it does not have, or even that it is in stock when it is not. In such circumstances, taking a stand on lying is a clear marker about yourself and the kind of work you will do. Asking the question, "Why can't we create a culture of truth here?" or "Why do we feel we have to lie?" could be the wise way to provoke change.

A TIME TO SPEAK, A TIME TO BE SILENT

Whatever your style or approach, you also run the risk of provoking wrath and retribution with your questions, -which brings us to another skill to tumble from this moment on the hill. The question was posed after a period of silence, as it was at least three hours since he spoke words of forgiveness, and he had only spoken twice in-between. There is a time for silence in such circumstances, therefore, and a time to speak out. You will need to weigh up in your mind whether you want to speak out, take a stand, and face whatever consequences may follow, or keep your own counsel, saving your words for another day.

I well remember a time when I was faced with a choice to make a powerful argument in favor of my position but risk losing my job and my family accommodation if I took my stand. I chose silence. In another context, I was faced with a massive locally organized opposition to my actions and I was invited to make my case in front of a national committee representing my employers. I chose to speak out whatever the consequences, although I had already made it clear that I was not going to say, "Back me or I quit!" I was not going to offer myself as a bargaining chip in the negotiation.

In each circumstance, I had to weigh up the potential cost and decide between silence or speech. Jesus of Nazareth had been silent for some time and is the moment came when it was the right time to speak. Although it was clearly spoken in a desperate moment, we know that it was not just a petulant shout because the question is a direct quotation from a poem written by the Jewish king David – one of Jesus' ancestors.[5] He was under extreme pressure but he still chose his words wisely.

A GOOD BOOK IN BAD TIMES

Here you get a glimpse of another of his skills, in the dark, which we will look at in more detail when we explore his last sentence. The skill is that is that of drawing wisdom and resources from the words of the

---

[5] Psalm 22:1

holy book that framed his life. There is an assumption in certain circles that old words and ancient wisdom are, at best, out of date, or at worst, redundant in today's world. What could it possibly have to say to an e-mail-driven, IT-based modern working culture?

When I faced my many accusers in the time of opposition I referred to earlier, I was invited to speak first. I had found a proverb that said, "The first to present a case seems right until another comes forward and asks questions."[6] I said that I would be happy to let my opponents speak first. I could see that the members of the committee who wanted to support me were beginning to wonder how I could defend myself in the face of the large body of evidence and growing set of arguments being laid out. I knew, however, that once the arguments had been heard, I would gently and firmly rebut each one and demonstrate my integrity, leaving my arguments, not those of my opponent, ringing in their ears. In the end, the ancient proverb was right. I was vindicated and thousands of lives have been changed as a result of the decisions that followed.

When he faced his darkest hours, Jesus of Nazareth turned to the wisdom of his spiritual heritage and the holy book which he had absorbed from childhood. If you read modern management books, you will notice that they are often littered with biblical quotations. This is testament to the fact that the words Jesus read, and those he spoke, have always contained timeless wisdom for today's racers.

WHY WAS HE ALONE?

Coming back to the specific quotation that Jesus spoke from his treasured holy book, you can now engage with his question by asking

---

6   Proverbs 18:17

why he was alone at this point. Why does he appear to be treading a God-forsaken path in total isolation? I suggest to you that the answers will provide you with a priceless skill set to add to your survival skills to help you navigate any part of your race when the going becomes extremely tough. Using this scenario of Jesus in turmoil as an illustration, I will try to describe this skill set for you now. So again, let's consider why he was alone during this time.

First, he was alone because there was no one else who could do this. You have already seen that this teacher had a deep sense of personal mission. He had concluded that he should lay down his life as a ransom to re-connect humanity with God. He knew that there was no one else qualified to do this job and it was, literally, his alone to do.

Just as the ability to balance your life is connected to having a personal sense of mission, the ability to stand alone for what is right is linked to your grasp of the uniqueness of your mission. There may come a point when you realize that the circumstances are such that you have to act and no one can do this for you. If we need to name this skill I would call it, "Seizing your uniqueness."

The circumstances that surround your "seizing" could be related to your position. You may hold a job in an organization that gives you a unique insight into a process or a project. Like Christoph Meili, you may have become privy to some startling information simply because of the post you hold in the business. You can see something that no one else can see.

At this point, let me suggest to you that being the lone voice may be challenging, but it can also be seen as a great privilege. It is possible to find yourself thinking that you are the only one in your team, group, or entire organization who holds certain values or beliefs. Far from discouraging you, it can be viewed as a privileged responsibility to be the voice of good news, the promoter of best practice, and even the whisperer of paradise in your place of work. It may even be the reason you are there at all.

Your vision doesn't have to be focused on the negative. It might be that you can see a huge gap in the market which, if filled, will benefit many people. Generally speaking, however, the type of vision we are exploring here is that which spots the flaw, injustice, or disaster in the system and realizes that something must be done. Jesus of Nazareth saw people imprisoned in their self-destructive behavior and set out to provide another way, a deeper truth, and a more vibrant life. His mission told him that he alone could do it, and his vision showed him that it had to be done.

Don't be lulled into thinking that he had no concerns about the aloneness he was facing. In the hours before he was arrested and as the last drama unfolded, his friend John overheard him saying, "If it is possible, let this cup pass away from me."[7] In other words, he was saying, "This is so hard for me. Isn't there some other way to do this?" But he concluded that it was not possible. He knew he had to do it and he knew he had to do it alone.

NO OTHER WAY?

The settlement of this conclusion reveals another profound underlying element in this rich seam of truth. What if there is no other route to reality and rescue except that which includes struggle and pain? Far from rejecting this route, his race seems to indicate that he could not fulfill his life's purpose without embracing this pain. Consequently, you can learn here a fact that you have already observed: You will not be able to fulfill your life's purpose without pain and struggle and

---

[7]   Matthew 26:39

suffering. There is no painless route to results. This is a high-price-high-reward dynamic. It may not lessen your pain, but it will help you to keep your eyes toward the light as you walk in the dark. If we need to name this one, we might call it "Embracing the pain."

We are still engaging with the question, "Why was he alone?" so let's look at another aspect of the answer. Jesus of Nazareth made his 33-year life's aim to be true to himself, his values, and his mission, even if that meant alienating some people and making enemies. He would describe this behavior as aiming to please his Father. He did not set out to make enemies, irritate the crowd, or court controversy; he simply held his focus on his calling.

Paradoxically, this teacher had an amazing ability to please people and exceed their expectations. Throughout his public life, he excited and delighted the crowds. But pleasing people was not his aim, he heard their applause but he was listening to a higher voice. It has been said that the world has yet to see what can be achieved by a person who truly does not worry about what people think of them. In the historical moment that we're discussing, perhaps the world had seen it and was witnessing the consequences of a person who was determined to operate out of his values and not pander to the crowd.

Psychologists will confirm that having a sense of higher calling and following it through is vital to mental health. You may race day to day, but when your terrain becomes hostile, you need to know that this pain has a purpose and there are reasons why you got to this lonely spot in the first place. The energy of purpose will empower you to keep going straight ahead when the easier, people-pleasing scenic routes seem so appealing.

In Jesus' dark situation, he was alone because he knew who he wanted to please and would not compromise to gain popular approval. I warned you that things would tumble out from the darkness. If we can now see clearly enough, we could label this skill "Knowing who you serve."

THE WORST OF TIMES

If you are going to plumb the depths of this moment, then you need to recognize that this was the worst experience of the carpenter's life. This wasn't just a difficult time; it was as bad as it could be.

As you read my words, think about the worst thing you have experienced thus far in your life. Maybe it was a bankruptcy, a divorce, or bereavement. It may have been a work-related experience of sustained bullying or financial crisis, or it could have been a health issue or an episode of unpleasant rejection and failure. To think about such times can give you a strange sensation as you bring memories to the front of your mind. It might be that healing and restoration has taken place and you can look back with some detachment, or it might be that your worst time is yet to come. Either way, let's attempt to draw some life-giving water from this deep well of the carpenter's experience by describing it in a little more detail. Maybe more things will emerge from the dark.

DEALING WITH THE INEVITABLE

There comes a point during a difficult and painful process when you can see what's coming next. How far in advance you can see depends on the nature of the circumstances, but eventually, you can observe an inevitable outcome. You don't need to be a clairvoyant or intelligence analyst to predict these outcomes; you just need to be observant – just watch.

For example, with the benefit of experience, you can predict that certain business decisions will definitely lead to bankruptcy or failure. Some clear symptoms of a disease indicate the definite arrival of incapacity, disability, or even death. At such times, people use fateful phrases such as, "Only a miracle can save us now." In moments like these, you are not just dealing with struggle. You are also dealing with the anticipation of struggle.

To expand your understanding of the moment of Jesus' struggle, consider the fact that, according to the biblical narrative and examples of his mystical nature, Jesus had anticipated the arrival of this time for many years, possibly most of his life. He had lived with an acute awareness that this would be his fate, and he regularly predicted its arrival to his team. Realizing this sharpens our focus of what he said in his sermon on the mount when he urged "Do not worry about tomorrow."[8] In the light of what we now know about his "tomorrows," which followed after he spoke these words, he was demonstrating a remarkable dignity in the face of his own future and was inviting you to learn that same dignity as you journey into your own darkness. The anticipation of pain is a challenging experience, but what I am suggesting is that the carpenter can teach you to enter the dark tunnel while still racing with poise.

As we search the ground for more survival skills, let me encourage you to reflect on the fact that the darkest moment of Jesus' life was also a point in time when right and wrong battled and combined. What this means for you is that, when you are convinced of the rightness of your cause, you can be energized to take your stand and pay the price of aloneness.

But what if you are *not* convinced of the rightness of your cause? What if you are alone because you are in the wrong, have messed up, and

---

[8]   Matthew 6:34

made a catastrophic mistake?

WHAT IF YOU'RE WRONG?

To show you how you can draw strength from the carpenter on the cross during your doubts, I need to describe a family phenomenon for you with which you may be familiar. Numerous families adopt the behavior of dumping their anger on one particular member. All kinds of blame, accusation, criticisms, and insults are regularly thrown at this individual as the rest of the family seems to be operating with some unwritten code designed to transfer all their pent-up frustration onto this unfortunate victim. Some psychologists call this behavior "scapegoating." The actual term originates from an ancient Jewish rite in which a high priest, a representative of the nation of Israel, confessed to God all the sins of the nation while placing his hands on a goat that stood as a symbolic surrogate between him and God. It was understood that the goat received all the nation's sins and then was sent to wander alone in the wilderness.[9]

Similarly, the modern-day human scapegoat is on the receiving end of an array of accusations, half-truths, and venom, and is expected to carry or absorb this array on behalf of the rest. The scapegoated individual will soon find that their own soul is polluted and they really do feel guilty as charged. In some scapegoating families, the behavior doesn't cease, even when the scapegoated individual is obviously wounded.

This is what was happening to Jesus on that dark hill in Jerusalem. Jesus of Nazareth was being scapegoated on a massive scale. He had endured 18 hours of sustained attack, and every kind of anger,

---

[9] Leviticus 16:20-22

accusation, and venom had been hurled at him. He knew what it was like to be alone and feel wrong – not his own wrong, but that of others, like the victimized scapegoat. Yet, at the same time, he was alone because he was right. He had not compromised, broken laws, or failed in any way. He was in the right, but he was willingly sacrificing himself to make things right for everyone else.

So now you can understand that there is a man who knows what it is like to be alone and right while simultaneously being alone and feeling wrong. More importantly, he understands your experience when you find yourself alone, right or wrong. He is now whispering another echo of paradise into your soul by saying to you, "I know what it is like," and, "I understand." This is an important point, because one of the greatest features of aloneness is the sense of being totally misunderstood. So Jesus now brings to you the gift of exquisite understanding as you race in the dark. It's a gift you can use as part of your survival repertoire and it is, like so many good gifts, quite a surprise.

TRUSTED WITH ABSENCE

To capture more wisdom from Jesus' "Isn't there another way?" question, consider the dynamic of parenting and letting children go. There comes a time when, as any parent knows, you have to let your child do something on his or her own. There is the first unsupervised journey or first time home alone. As the years go by, wise parents will learn to trust their children with a feeling of parental absence, and this is essential if real maturity is to be achieved.

When you re-visit your darkest moments, you may recognize that they were hallmarked with a feeling of absence. Not only were you alone, but you probably felt an awareness of withdrawal. This strange experience has been called the *dark night of the soul*.[10] It is a time of emptiness, dryness, or aching isolation in which every light seems to have switched off and all that once nourished you has disappeared. Yet without such experiences of being trusted with absence, you will not be able to mature. The absence is not a malicious hiding but a loving release in order to promote your well being. It can be seen as a rite of passage that qualifies you to call yourself mature.

The question that pierced the darkness that day was surely the result of Jesus of Nazareth experiencing his own dark night of the soul. It's almost too mysterious to describe, but something happened in that moment. Whatever it was, it resulted in a complete and radical identification with your humanity, and somehow, it powerfully qualified him to empathize with the universal human experience of separation. Up until this point, he had not known what you and I have tasted so frequently – a sense of separation from the Father. At that moment, he knew, and therefore he cried out in his feeling of ultimate separation from his Father. So he has been there and fought an epic battle. And as we will see later on in our race, he won not just the battle, but the wisdom to speak to your soul.

This moment was a turning point in the six hour epic of Jesus' crossing his finish line. Numerically, it is the fourth sentence that serves as a window for observing the principles by which this man mastered his life's race. As you look through the next three sentence-windows, you will see an approaching finish where changes occur and issues begin to resolve. From this fourth lesson, we saw the reality that Jesus knew all along: Dark moments are regularly turning points when something moves, changes, or begins to emerge to break a pattern and transform

---

[10] A concept first described by St. John of the Cross. It can be found in *The Collected Works of St. John of the Cross*, Kieran Kavanaugh and Otilio Rodriguez, trans., (I C S Publications, Institute of Carmelite St.; Revised edition, January 1, 1991).

the race. As you look back on your difficult times, you may recognize how the nature of certain turning points made it so that your life and work were never quite the same after such experiences.

This is what countless racers over the centuries have experienced, and this is another reason why the man who changed the world can still change the way you work. Century after century, your predecessors have raced into the dark and found themselves alone. They have drawn comfort from the carpenter who had been through his hardest hour, cried out his most demanding question, and held on until the darkness passed. I hope that you too can now draw on that same comfort until the darkness passes. And yes, it *will* pass, so hold on.

LAP FIVE:
BEING YOURSELF –
THE OBVIOUS HEART

What would you do if you were faced with the task of delivering a two-hour presentation on the subject of personal development to a group of about 100 young ladies of 17 and 18 years of age? This was my challenge when I was asked to visit my daughter's former high school as a guest speaker. I approached this challenge thinking about the most common issue that cropped up in one-to-one coaching sessions when I work with people in their 30s, 40s and 50s. In my preparation, I tried to pick out one theme that would be really useful for these young ladies to explore and engage with now, so they could gain some early expertise in predicting their own challenges.

To focus my mind, I asked myself a series of questions: (1) What is the most common struggle, pain, blockage, or problem that people bring into their coaching? (2) What is the most repeated, common frustration that my clients have experienced 10, 20, or 30 years further into their race than these young ladies? (3) Could I capture that experience and make it useful for my 100-strong, somewhat daunting, audience?

As I let my mind wander and my thoughts simmer, something bubbled up to the surface and revealed that the most common struggle was that people simply did not feel comfortable in their own skins. They would not necessarily have used these exact words, but the symptoms were clear. Work, life, projects, and experiences had distorted the shape of their personalities, molding them into unsatisfactory expressions of their true selves. Having to put on a show, live up to expectations, or play a game for so long had worn them down, leaving them wondering who they really were. The grand drama of the market had forced them to take on roles that did not fit with their own styles and character traits. This caused them to develop personas in order to please their peers or employers, while forgetting their own preferred lines. In short, they had spent a large proportion of their working days putting on an act.

Swirling around in a vortex of mixed motives, these individuals found themselves driven by fear, greed, jealously, the desire to impress, and seeking approval while not really enjoying applause. With such mantras as, "If you can't stand the heat, get out of the kitchen," ringing in their ears, the pressure to perform or to be written out of the plot further distorted any expressions of authenticity.

WELCOME TO THE REAL WORLD

The irony of this is that the marketplace in general, and work in particular, is often called "the real world." This real world seems to be populated by people pretending, acting, and performing in a sort of conspiracy of unreality designed to make sure the show goes on. Just think about our widespread use of phrases such as, "What role do you play in your company?" or "Let's have a performance review," and you'll understand my point.

So, after all, I found a way of communicating this issue for 100 young ladies. They applauded my lecture and their tutors were pleased. I suspect some of them will still turn up for coaching 20 years later with this struggle on their agendas, but hopefully a few will take my warnings to heart and make some wise choices now, before they succumb to the unreality of the marketplace drama.

My task now, however, is to find a way of communicating something of value to you as you race so you can find your own authentic running style, which will be characterized by being comfortable in your own skin. To achieve this, you must explore a little further into the nature of the challenge you are facing. Because the problem arises, not by a sudden fall from reality into acting, but from a subtle descent down a series of small steps taken over time. And this gradual process eventually leads to an uneasy awareness that all is not as it should be. So how do you explore your path and become more aware of the slope you may be on?

You can assess your personal profile in this matter by asking whether you really are able to be yourself at work. Do you feel like you have to be a different person when you are at work, adopting a set of behaviors and mannerisms that, if you are honest, is not an accurate reflection of who you really are?

The difficulty in answering these questions arises because the habits you have formed may have become so ingrained in your character that you can't always identify the real you in the crowd. On top of that, there are some specific cultural behaviors that you may adopt, such as wearing a particular type of clothes or employing jargon-filled language that you are comfortable with at work, even though you abandon these behaviors when you leave. So they may be a part of your real self even though they exist at the margins of your taste and style.

Sometimes, however, the pressure to perform builds up to sufficient levels and starts to ring all kinds of personal alarms in your mind, triggering stressful reactions throughout your being. This occurs when there is a serious mismatch between who you are and what you are being asked to do. This is a very familiar phenomenon in stress-management circles because it regularly leads to dissatisfied, unhappy, and unfulfilled working experiences that leave people disillusioned and discouraged.

PEGS AND HOLES

A creative artist who is burdened with administrative tasks. A middle manager who is promoted to leader. A teacher forced to handle budgets. A loner asked to work in an open-plan office. These are just a few of a million possible examples of mismatch. For you, it could be that there is a partial mismatch, whereby the balance of your work is such that you spend too low a percentage of your time doing the things you excel at, are trained for, and love. If you find yourself saying, "This is not what I signed up for," "It's getting harder to express my views," or, "I find my work more draining than nourishing," then you may be suffering under the symptoms of mismatch.

Further confusion may be created if you do not really have a clear idea of your own strengths, style, and working tastes. If you are a little disconnected from yourself in terms of understanding your true nature, then it will compound the challenge to be yourself, owing to the fact that you don't really know yourself.

So the marketplace is littered with individuals living with various levels of disillusionment, ranging from subconscious anxiety to painfully obvious awareness. Have a look at these words from Frederick Buechner:

This world is full of people who seem to have listened to the wrong voice and are now engaged in life-work in which they find no pleasure or purpose and who run the risk of suddenly realizing someday that they have spent the only years that they are ever going to get in this world doing something which could not matter less to themselves or to anyone else. This does not mean, of course, people who are doing work that from the outside looks unglamorous and humdrum, because obviously such work as that may be a crucial form of service and deeply creative. But it means people who are doing work that seems simply irrelevant, not only to the great human needs and issues of our time but also to their own, need to grow and develop as humans.[1]

Beuchner's observation opens up the other side of this challenge – that living with mismatch for too long will lead to a long-term regret, – or to put it more positively, discovering a true match will lead to lifelong

---

[1] Frederick Beuchner, *The Hungering Dark* (Harper San Francisco, 1985), 29.

release and satisfaction.

Composer and musician Howard Goodhall once presented a TV series on the great 20th century composers. In it, he commented that there were composers who achieved enormous popularity in their own lifetimes by writing what people wanted to hear. The truly great composers, he concluded, were the ones who wrote what they wanted – or needed – to write as an expression from within themselves. So the question before you could be, "Who will write your music?" Or, if you prefer, "Who will sing your song?" Or, "Who will dance your dance?"

THE LIFELONG QUESTION

These questions express themselves in every stage of your life. When you are young, you ask, "What should I do?" When you are in the middle laps of your race, you ask, "Am I doing the right thing?" And in the closing laps, you ask, "Have I done the right thing? Did I run well? Did I make a difference? Was it worth it?"

This brings us back to the closing laps of the carpenter-teacher's race. We will now encounter the fifth phrase he spoke as he crossed his finish – a phrase which gives you a window into the issues of reality, authenticity, and being true to yourself.

At first sight, the phrase does not appear to provide much information, but first sight is generally not the best option when observing these moments. These moments always invite you to look deeper. The phrase in question consists of just three English words:

"I am thirsty."[2]

---

[2] John 19:28

This was a moment of raw physicality when the brute facts of his experiences were breaking through into his words as he battled with the limitations of his body. In short, it was a moment of stark reality. All subtlety was stripped away, leaving an expression of authentic humanity at its most vulnerable. Here, as throughout our visit to this hill, you must remember that he was at work, and he delivered his expression of thirst while he was working on his greatest project and highest calling. So we are looking at this exposed moment in the context of working environments to learn the lessons for your race, bearing in mind that there is always more going on than what first appears.

NOTHING BUT THE TRUTH...

On an immediate level, this phrase was an expression of authenticity simply because it was true. He said he was thirsty because he was thirsty. One of the central physiological features of Roman crucifixion was that the victim suffered a raging thirst, far beyond usual day-to-day experiences. It's just a fact, totally in keeping with how he expressed his values throughout his life. For example, on another hill at another time, he said to his hearers, "Let your 'yes' be 'yes' and your 'no' be 'no.'"[3] London financial market traders have a motto that contains identical sentiments, "My word is my bond."

To express simple honesty as you work is a disarming characteristic; it is simultaneously gentle and powerful. Please remember that we are on a quest to discover and release the best expression of who you are, the authentic version of you as you were designed. And in the moment when he admitted his thirst, the carpenter was inviting you to adopt the same transparent honesty that he displayed.

---

[3] Matthew 5:37 (The Sermon on The Mount)

While we're addressing the subject, it is worth reflecting on the flip-side of the lesson and noting the damage that dishonesty creates. The trouble with bending the truth at work is that you risk bending your character out of shape. Little by little, you learn to live a lie and the damage becomes harder to undo. It can start with a simple statement such as, "Sorry I'm late, but the train was delayed," when the reality is that you knowingly caught a train that was very unlikely to get you to work on time. So your statement is not strictly true; your tardiness was also due to your choices. This trivial example illustrates the point precisely because it is trivial. It is made of the same material as the statement, "We cannot lend you money to buy this business due to market conditions," when the reality is that money has become tight because of corrupt corporate greed, malpractice, and unregulated institutions. So you must realize that, at its most basic level, being authentic is built on a commitment to being truthful.

A very good friend of mine was overseeing the purchase of a company. For legitimate reasons, he was having a bit of trouble raising the funds for this purchase. He had to make a call to the CEO of this company to explain the delay. In complete honesty, he simply explained that it was taking a little longer to raise the funds than he expected, but that he hoped to have them in place soon. The CEO's response was, "Thank you for telling me the truth; I will wait for you to raise the funds because I want to work with someone who is honest." The deal later went through.

Rather then ring up with some stalling story about lawyers and due diligence, or some fictitious flaw in the negotiations that were holding up proceedings, my friend chose to risk jeopardizing the multi-million dollar deal rather than avoid the truth. Telling a CEO that you are having trouble raising funds to buy his company could easily panic him into pulling out. In this case, the truth remained the chosen path. I use the words "chosen path" quite deliberately here because my company-purchasing friend did not just decide on the spur of the moment to employ truth on a temporary contract. His truthful approach was borne out of a lifelong commitment to truth, that commitment simply showed itself in his business practices. The fact is that the matter was settled in his mind long before the conversation of disclosure with the CEO.

There are also other aspects of truthfulness worth including here in our reflections. Sometimes truthfulness means saying, "I am angry" or, "I am disappointed" or, "I am optimistic" or, "I am not going to do that project in that way." Here the truthfulness is an accurate and open expression of a reaction to certain circumstances. Again, the flipside is helpful when you consider how often you can be tempted to tell a subtle lie hidden in the words, "I'm fine." The truth is that you're not fine at all, and each lie kills a little part of your soul, taking you another tiny step away from authenticity.

We could illustrate this point a thousand times but that would not add to its simple message: 'Yes' should mean 'yes' and 'no,' 'no.' Authenticity means telling the truth, unembellished, unbent, and unadorned – it's a foundation of reality.

NEED IS GOOD

Looking again at Jesus' phrase, you can see that, "I am thirsty" is an admission of need and a request for help. There is an intriguing irony on display here, because one of the metaphors that Jesus of Nazareth used to describe his work was that of a dispenser of living water, designed to satisfy all thirst so completely that the recipient would "never thirst again."[4] He cast himself quite deliberately in the role of thirst quencher, and millions of racers over hundreds of years have

---

[4] John 4:13

testified to the deep satisfaction they experience when drawing on this living water for their own thirsty souls. Yet he was prepared to admit to his own thirst as he carried out his work. It is not weak to be thirsty; it's just human and normal. The confusion where you work probably creeps in when the prevailing culture almost unconsciously dictates that you are not allowed to express aspects of humanity because they might imply weakness, without acknowledging that these aspects are, in fact, perfectly normal. So the result of such a culture is a developed habit of hiding or pretending.

Shakespeare's observation that, "All the world's a stage"[5] could be applied to such working cultures. If you keep playing your part this way, you may find that you lose the ability to seek proper support, and to keep the image intact, you end up performing poorly as a result. So you may play the part of confidence, competence, and control when you are, in fact, struggling with an over-complicated workload. You may play the part of the joker in order to hide your anxieties, or you may play the part of a leader when you know you are much more effective in a supporting role.

This type of play acting at work soon leads to the problems presented in the coaching sessions I described earlier. The problems show themselves once you realize that you have worked your way into a role that you simply don't fit.

It takes a great deal of courage to admit need and ask for help. Once summoned, however, that courage illustrates a profound inner strength and releases the truth that everybody already knows: None of us is as smart as all of us. If you express need and ask for help, you empower people around you without disempowering yourself. You invite them to bring their strengths and resources to bear on the problem and solve

---

5 William Shakespeare, *As You Like It*, Act II, Scene VII, Line 139

it with you. If you refuse to acknowledge your needs, you run the risk of isolation, which leads to ostracism, and instead of gaining respect, you lose it.

Throughout his work, Jesus of Nazareth invited his team to share the workload. Given what we know about his competence and skills, this is remarkable. If anyone could have done it all, it was likely to have been him. But he was a real human being who deliberately limited himself as part of his authentic expression of reality. In his finish-line moment, he had limited himself so drastically that his body was screaming out in thirst, and he needed a drink. He had made himself vulnerable and invited someone to help.

I would suggest to you that the best expressions of authentic humanity are truthful, courageous, and vulnerable at the same time – not as a charade, but because that combination corresponds to reality – that's the way it is.

Of course, let's not be naive here. I am not suggesting that you go to work and spend large proportions of your day exposing provocative truths or divulging deep personal information in a quest to express your true feelings. You will not keep your job for long if you do. Jesus of Nazareth was very adept at handling double-meaning questions, defeating the cynical comments, and avoiding revealing his views when that revelation would be, in his own words, "throwing pearls to pigs."[6] He was the one who advised his team to be "as shrewd as snakes and as innocent as doves,"[7] and he was the one who used carefully crafted stories to wrap around his message so that only the serious inquirers would do the unwrapping work to discover his meanings. He was no novice at subtlety and not to be taken for a ride by underhand

---

[6] Matthew 7:6

[7] Matthew 10:16

schemers. But his strategies were always honest, and his methods were consistent as he refused to play the game of deceit or dance the dance of manipulation. For him, acting was hypocrisy and hypocrisy was the act that made him more angry than almost anything else. This leads us into another valuable glimpse through the window of the words, "I am thirsty."

THIRSTING FROM THE INSIDE OUT

As I've indicated before, one of my specialties is human physiology, so while researching this material, I analyzed the physiology of thirst. It is a complex process involving the brain, kidneys, hormones, and blood. Although the sensation may be that of a dry throat or mouth, thirst is a multi-faceted inner dynamic. It is also an illustration of an aspect of reality worth exploring. Thirst is an expression of what is going on inside. The complex physiology leads to an experienced sensation that is then expressed in words. To put it another way, there is a consistency, or congruence, between what is happening inside, how it is being experienced, and what is said. The reality is going from the inside out.

You have had moments of congruence even if you didn't describe them this way. Think of a time when you felt you were at your best, really buzzing, achieving, exhilarated, and fulfilled. In these moments, there is a connection between your understanding of yourself, your experiences, and your expression. For example, if you believe yourself to be a musician and you hear music in your head and you then express it through singing, playing, or writing, all these components come together. If you are a doctor and you are passionate about healing, you make a great diagnosis and carry it through to seeing a patient recover, you experience congruence.

Jesus of Nazareth understood himself to be the light of the world. He enlightened people and he said that he was the light. There was a harmony between who he was, who he understood himself to be, how he experienced himself, and what he said and did. His life was an illustration of the fact that the best expressions of reality come from deep within and work their way out into your life.

This is in contrast to many work experiences where you are asked to respond to an external agenda and conform to a job specification designed to fit a set of tasks, not necessarily your individual skills. Your best work will always emerge out of who you are and cannot be imposed on you from the outside. Describing his work, Yehudi Menuhin, one of the world's greatest violinists, used the phrase, "For this I came." He used to illustrate the connection, in his mind, between his vocation and his identity.

You already know that, whatever work you do, it will be the "you" who does it, and you will always want to do it your way. The problems arise when you are constrained and confined, being forced to conform to an alien style. You will still achieve, but not as much or as purposefully as you could.

I am not saying that you can necessarily get all this from the three words, "I am thirsty." What I am saying is that this phrase is a powerful physiological illustration of the point. And if you look through the words back into the carpenter's race, you can find further wisdom to corroborate this illustration.

DESIGNER LABELS

The more I study physiology, the more I find myself marveling at the intricacy of the human body. Thirst is one illustration, but there are millions more that combine to produce you as an individual that the old Jewish writers described as "fearfully and wonderfully made."[8] This can be seen as another aid to following in the footsteps of Jesus of Nazareth, who embraced his humanity and celebrated its design. One of his followers quotes him as describing himself to his Father as, "A body you prepared for me."[9] He saw his humanity as a brilliantly crafted, specially prepared living entity full of well-designed parts. I can put it like this: Our bodies are full of designer labels.

The powerful connection with your quest for reality becomes clear when you consider yourself as being designed and then celebrate that reality. Your quest for reality then becomes a journey of self-discovery that deepens your understanding of how you are individually designed, which then helps you to more effectively work out of who you really are. Put simply, the more you know about your design, the more you can fulfill the purpose for which you are designed and be your best expression of authentic humanity. You may then find that you can go to work celebrating your humanity rather than pretending to be someone else.

If you're not at that point of authenticity just yet, one of the reasons that you may not currently feel comfortable in your own skin could be that you don't really value your skin. You find it difficult to appreciate how wonderfully made you really are. You may have started to agree with voices that remind you of your obvious shortcomings or observe your inabilities to achieve. You may have developed a sense of perfectionism and a nagging thought that you can never realize your potential or live up to the expectations in your mind. You may feel this is a personal struggle, but I can assure you that you are a part of a large population sharing this internal struggle. Many individuals walk around with a self-critical voice in their heads telling them to, "Try

---

[8] Psalm 139:14

[9] Hebrews 10:5

harder! Do better! Pull your socks up!" It is a parental voice demanding higher, faster, larger, and greater achievements!, Or it is a peer whisper saying, "Compete. Conform. Get style." It is the voice from TV commercials saying, "Lose weight! Look great! Earn more! Buy this and you will be happy!" It is an imaginary preacher saying, "Behave! Provide! Cooperate! Serve! Purify!" When these voices are in unison, the choral theme they chant is:

Don't be this, be that.
Don't do this, do that.
You're always not quite good enough,
But try to live up to all our expectations.

When you take your choir to work, it urges you to please or to obsess and achieve. You will work yourself hard to quiet the sound. And the training department accompanies the choir by adopting the strategy that, if you are not good at something, then you might benefit from training in that area. So millions of dollars are invested in the project of getting you to focus on your weaknesses and join in with the choir.

The one thing this choir will not sing is a song of celebration. In the name of humility, such songs would seem inappropriate and arrogant. So the result in you is a constant striving after other people's images of who you should be and what you should do, while devaluing your own design and distancing you from both an understanding and appreciation of your authentic self. The result is that you miss out on the party of you and bypass the legitimate and releasing celebrations of your fearfully and wonderfully made character, style, and personality.

So perhaps it's time for me to give you some invitations which, if you accept, will enable you to come to your own party, meet the real you, and find genuine fun in the process.

YOU ARE WARMLY INVITED...

The party to which I am inviting you does not require a fancy dress, tuxedo, or ball gown – it is a come-as-you-are event. If you look at the self-awareness sentences that Jesus of Nazareth used to describe his identity, there are a number of other phrases prior to "I am thirsty" that also start with the words, "I am." There are at least seven famous ones including, "I am the light of the world," and "I am the Good Shepherd." In using such language, he is deliberately evoking a moment in history that had been indelibly etched in the minds of his hearers. They all knew of the time reported in their own holy writings of the meeting between Moses and his God. In their ancient writings, the title God used to describe himself was "I AM WHO I AM."[10] It is the ultimate expression of inner security. There is a serenity, completeness, and integration about the phrase with no pretension, anxiety, or agitation. It is a matter-of-fact statement of being and a disarming description of unapologetic reality.

To understand the power of this self-description, compare it with how you, or people you know, would finish a sentence that starts with, "I am...." You usually add your job title, "I am a teacher," "I am a lawyer," or, "I am a builder." You may want to listen to your internal choir that says, "I am jealous," "I am insecure," or, "I am not as good as you." Or perhaps your internal voice says, "I am better than you,", or, "I am richer than you." These last statements, being apparently self-confident, still contain an inherent insecurity around the sense that simply being who you are, on its own, is not acceptable.

Consider how often you find yourself driven by motivation that could be phrased, "I am trying to please," "I am striving for perfection," or, "I am determined to improve." Alternatively, you may be driven to

---

[10] Exodus 3:14

despair with, "I am a failure," "I am incompetent," or, "I am unattractive" ringing in your ears.

One of the restorative activities of the carpenter is to run beside you in your race and teach you to become aware that being yourself is acceptable. You don't have to be anything or anyone else, nor do you have to apologize, justify, or explain when describing yourself. True authenticity is a journey that takes you step by step towards the ability to say, "I am who I am," not with capital letters, proclaiming yourself to be divine, but with small letters, revealing the image of your designer in every aspect of your brilliantly crafted being.

In order to take this journey towards a place of peace where you can own the phrase *I am who I am* for yourself, you will need to keep doing the work of getting to know yourself. "An unexamined life," according to Socrates, "is not worth living." This is a sentiment that would have been shared by a man named James, who was Jesus' younger brother. Almost certainly a fellow carpenter who worked with his brother in the family business, James wrote a letter to individuals around his region reminding them, among other things, to stay self-aware. He illustrated his point by explaining the absurdity of looking in a mirror and then promptly turning away and forgetting what you look like.[11] The mirror he had in mind was the sacred words of faith contained in the Holy Bible. This is exactly what we are doing – by looking at these seven phrases spoken by Jesus of Nazareth, we are seeing models of reality that reflect light back into your soul. Put simply, the more you know yourself, the more you can be yourself, and consequently, the more you can celebrate rather than denigrate your identity.

---

[11] James 1:23-24

JUMPING INTO YOUR SKIN

At this point, I want to give you a few suggestions connected to my coaching experiences that have helped individuals jump into their own skin, so to speak, and find greater authenticity. The key is to engage in a number of questions that will open up your thinking and reveal your true self.

First, ask yourself what you have learned from life so far. Followers of the carpenter were called "learners" because the great challenge was to keep learning throughout their lives. By asking yourself what you have learned from your life, you will get some insight into how you have lived. For example, if you say, "I have learned that there is always a solution if I look," then you know that you have a tendency towards positive thinking, problem solving, and searching. If you say, "I have learned that life is full of challenges that require a great effort to meet," then you know that you tend to persevere and fight for what you believe in. The more you reflect on what you are learning, the more your life will speak back to you.

Secondly, ask what you hope to learn in the future. This will give you insight into your motivation and dreams. If you know you hope to learn to be more patient, this tells you something about your pace and your values. If you follow this question by considering what's stopping you from learning what you hope to learn, this will give you an understanding of your struggles.

You can tell a lot about Jesus of Nazareth by examining the reasons why people sought his company and asked his opinions. So ask yourself the questions, "What do people come to me for?" and, "What do they get when they come?" Interestingly, the carpenter who said, "I am thirsty," is also the one who invited others to come to him so that he could quench their thirsty souls with spiritual satisfaction. If people come to you for peace or affirmation, then you know that part of the meaning of your individual *I am who I am* is a person of peace.

Third, ask yourself what frustrates you. By visiting your frustrations, you can spy on your strong feelings and release an understanding of your passions, ambitions, and drives. If rudeness frustrates you, then you know that courtesy and civility matter greatly to you. If devaluing individuals irritates you, then you have spied on your care for human dignity.

Jesus of Nazareth did not often show anger, but when he did, he showed his soul. In the chapter on stress, you saw that his anger at the temple financial racket was motivated by what he saw as the commercialization of a place for people to pray their "Father prayers." If you look at his life story you will find that he was most angry when confronting hypocrisy or, in other words, inauthenticity. It was the arrogance of certain individuals who refused to say, "I am thirsty," that angered him and revealed his passions for reality.

VISIT THE BEST OF TIMES

To get even closer to understanding yourself, reflect on the times of your life when you were at your best. You have often heard it said that you can learn from your mistakes, but how often have you considered learning from your successes? Try to recall moments, projects, conversations, or days when you felt at your absolute best. What were you doing, how were you doing it, what were you thinking, and how did you feel? By visiting these times, you will meet the best expressions of your authentic design and learn to celebrate the skill of the designer as well as the intricacy of yourself.

When individuals with whom I have worked have visited these times with me, they have gained remarkable insights into their inherent design. And because of this, they have become very effective, positive forces within their spheres of influence. One person, for example, realized her giftedness could be described as "capturing voices." She is an individual who actively listens to the requests of clients and colleagues and then produces designed items (brochures, programs, posters, etc.) that delight those clients. This individual has effectively captured the meaning of her client's requests and personally taken meaningful ownership of the task. Consequently, this person regularly over-delivers so that people are exceptionally pleased with the results as she captures voices and turn people's words into beautiful designs.[11a] Others have discovered that they can deliver delight by exceeding all expectations in their homes and in their marketplaces, or that they can bring a fresh perspective to a project by finding angles, and showing people new truths.

One man came to realize that he is person of "shalom," who brings a sense of wholeness wherever he goes. To clarify, what I mean by shalom in this sense is not merely from the simple interpretation of the word "peace." Shalom is much more complex than an absence of conflict, and more than people simply being nice to each other. Shalom is a sense of transcendent wholeness. One who truly lives from a place of shalom experiences very deep completeness and contentment. They are driven by this core of wholeness and therefore live intentionally to share it with others, ushering them into a place of shalom that, as the bible puts it, "transcends all understanding."[12] This is a person who, often at great personal cost to himself, facilitates individuals and groups in such a way that many around him experience the profound complexity of shalom.

Another person has uncovered an ability to redeem fragmented stories and turn them into integrated narratives. The more these people look,

---

[11a] For you 'M' - just for you.

[12] Philippians 4:7

the more they discover that there is, right at the heart of their design, a unique dynamic that defines and releases them into the person they were born to be. The phrase I use to help people understand this phenomenon is "Catching the breath of God," because when they realize that there is uniqueness in their souls, they discover what has been breathed into them, and it energizes their whole being.

This is the road to reality – when the heart becomes obvious, open, and available. If you regularly implement these exercises, you will see who you are, celebrate it, and consciously operate out of your core design, enjoying the freedom to be the most authentic expression of yourself.

As you can see, "I am thirsty" is a powerful expression of authentic human reality, and you have looked through the window of its wisdom to see how the carpenter embraced his humanity. However, to be true to this moment, you also need to hear the low notes as well as the high ones. For this moment is also one of extreme suffering, and it is possible to forget that suffering is also a part of reality. There are three important observations that will help you grasp the painful side of this phrase. Once we combine them with your other learning, your search for authenticity will approach completeness. I wish I could explain authenticity and avoid the issue of suffering, but that would betray the passion of these truths and only lead to a partial reality. Here are the three observations:

First, suffering is not meaningless. The thirst of Jesus, as well as the six hours of struggling around it, was part of his work and mission. His suffering enabled him to do his job. In fact, it was intrinsic to his job. You already know that if you adopt a particular attitude to your suffering, it will help create, develop, and purify your character. Suffering, if you let it, strips away the persona and reveals the person.

This is why James advised you to consider struggles as pure joy,[13] not because you enjoy them, but because, when you take that view, it does the work of removing the layers of unreality.

Second, suffering is never permanent – it will pass. When you are in the middle of it, pain seems to slow everything down. But the carpenter taught his learners that joy would follow as certainly as a new born baby's cry obliterates the pain of birth.[14] This is vital for you to hold onto at work, in life, and in death, because this carpenter is teaching us how to work, live, and die – it's about the whole race.

Lastly, suffering is never more than you can bear. There is always an eventual way out. Jesus' best friend, who watched him die, later wrote that God will eventually wipe away all tears.[15]

If you pause and reflect on our race together so far, you can now see how Father prayers, skills of forgiveness, whispers of paradise, living in moments, and standing alone are all complementary gifts from the carpenter on the hill. These gifts combine to reveal the generosity of his spirit and the power of his work. His heart is becoming obvious and he is slowly helping you to take yourself – the real you – with you wherever you go, especially to work.

---

[13] James 1:2

[14] John 16:21

[15] Revelation 21:4

LAP SIX:
GETTING THINGS DONE –
THE REAL DEAL

Pause a moment and think back to your greatest achievements and proudest times. Take your mind to the completion of a project, the passing of an exam, or the acquisition of your heart's desire. Visit those stored memories of perfect days, reliable colleagues, and of winning something that mattered to you. Take some time to reflect on a job well done, a career path chosen, or a reward you received.

Sometimes the memory is of the spectacular, but just as often it is of the small victories and steps. As you revisit these good times, perhaps you can feel the exquisite satisfaction associated with getting something done. It is the climbing of a mountain and seeing the view. It is the leaping of a hurdle and surprising yourself at your strength. It is the scoring of a goal, home-run, or basket, and punching the air. It can be a quiet relief or even an exhausted collapse, and occasionally an actual anticlimax as the adrenaline eventually subsides. But when you have done it, got it, won it, bought it, beaten it, or survived it, there is almost always an ecstatic sense of achievement associated with doing what you set out to do.

Equally as intense is the agony of the opposite. I'm not talking about failure, because failure is an integral part of everyone's story and can be vital for progress. The opposite seems to be made of a million conspiring enemies marshalling forces to frustrate you and thwart your efforts. This is what happens when a delivery is delayed, an item is out of stock, a colleague misses a deadline, an employee defrauds you, a contract is lost, an opportunity missed, or a target not hit. A dream remains undreamt or unrealized, words are unsaid, investments unmade, and everything is incomplete. It is the lack of completion, wholeness, reliability, and integrity that results in no results, ends in loose ends, and satisfies no one.

Our task is to bottle the ecstasy of achievement and keep drinking from that as we attempt to analyze this powerful skill-set of getting things done.

BIG DEALS AND DAILY AGREEMENTS

More often than not, the framework surrounding achievement comes in the form of a contract or agreement. Interested parties decide that they want to deliver a result and divide up the cost, benefit, risks, and rewards by mutual consent, and then apportion responsibilities and tasks. Many such agreements operate in the background of your life while you get on with the day-to-day job at hand. So you have a contract with your employer in which you've agreed to sell your time and talents for an annual fee, called your salary, and then you start your job. Contracts are as varied as species of insects, but whether you are on an hourly or monthly rate, or on a short-term contract with a client, the principle remains the same.

With these large agreements ticking over in the background, you will enter into a multitude of micro-agreements every day. You may be able to count them as you go. You agree to write a report, make a phone call, keep an appointment, deliver a product, or provide a service. If you keep a record, you may be surprised at how many agreements you enter into each day, from filling a shopping cart and agreeing to pay the retailer, to engaging lawyers to help you buy a multi-million-dollar company, to bargaining with your teenage daughter about what time she will come home in the evening. Agreements to achieve are so fundamental to work and life that they could almost be seen as the building blocks of a career, or in the racing-rat language, paces taken along the track.

In this race of life, there are thousands of finishes, chalk lines on the ground, or plastic ribbons that you cross as you head steadily towards your very final moments. Each project has its finishes, each taskit's endings, each day closes, and each era ends. Life and work are full of finishes, and crammed into your race will be a collection of closures in the context of deals, relationships, contracts, and ultimately bereavements.

ENDING WELL

How then can you learn to end a project well, end a day well, end a task well, and end your life well? How can you come to healthy agreements that will provide the achievement infrastructure you need to build something of value? How can you keep crossing finish lines, breaking ribbons, and eventually climax in a triumphant exit at the end of a well-run race?

If ever there was a triumphant exit at the end of a well-run race, an ending of dignity and a closure of power, it is in that of our master racer, whose last six racing hours we have been examining. As you will shortly see, there are many closing lessons to be gathered from all of his last hours, but his sixth statement as he died specializes in teaching us about endings. Here is the quote as relayed by his best friend, John:

"When he had received the drink, Jesus said, 'It is finished'"[1]

Other friends add the detail that he spoke these words in a loud voice, which gives you another insight into why he received the drink, a reason that we talked about in the previous chapter. The bottom line is that he wanted some help, in the form of a drink, to get to this point of shouting out, "It is finished!" Knowing that it is a shout helps us understand the spirit of the words and learn the racing lessons.

ONE BIG WORD

This statement is three words in English, but it is one word (*tetelestai*) in the Greek language of the Bible, and that one word has a history. It was used when an artist signed off a painting – finished. The word was

---

[1] John 19:30

used when a servant reported back to his master that a job had been done – finished. Farmers used it to describe new-born animals in their pristine perfection. Athletes used it as a victory cry when they triumphantly crossed a finish line.

There is a clear note of celebration built into the melody of this word, and Jesus deliberately used this tone to ring out his assertive self-expression. The paradox is that, in the context of extraordinarily difficult and painful work, there is a moment of celebration. So startling is the presence of this celebration that you can only conclude it was meant to be there to wake us up to its importance.

I am suggesting to you that building regular celebrations of achievement into your race is vital for your health and well-being and an aid in your ability to get things done. The man nicknamed The Great Dissenter, Oliver Wendall Holmes, put it like this:

"The riders in the race do not stop when they reach the goal. There is a little finishing canter before coming to a standstill. There is time to hear the kind voices of friends and say to oneself, 'The work is done.'"[2]

His expression echoes an earlier and even greater dissenter dying on a hill who shouts, "Finished!" in the face of achievement.

So the question it poses to you is, "Have you learned to pause and celebrate, or are you so intent on racing on that you miss the milestones along the way?" When you pass an exam, gain a qualification, close a deal, land a job or a contract, finish a project, reach your year-end or gain a promotion, there is a time to celebrate. It's a legitimate and necessary dynamic designed to honor your progress. It is neither

---

[2] http://en.thinkexist.com/quotation/the_riders_in_a_race_do_not_stop_when_they_reach/148877.html

humility to forget your achievements nor arrogance to remember them; it is merely appropriate and wise.

So enjoy the kind voices, raise a glass of champagne, receive your medal, and enjoy a job well done, slowly canter to a standstill, and then move on with new energy in your soul derived from the activity of healthy celebration.

MULTIPLE FINISHES

Further inspection of this closing moment reveals that it contains multiple finishes happening simultaneously. In keeping with the character of the six hours we are examining, there are concentrated lessons compacted into each event just waiting for us to open up and take with us as we race. We will try to open them one at a time, even though they may merge as the opening process continues.

This finish that we are examining was obviously the finish of a life well lived. Almost immediately after these words, Jesus breathes his last and his life is over. Stephen Covey, in his best seller on the habits of effective people, proposes a mental exercise in which you take yourself to an imaginary funeral and listen to the words of a friend, family member, and co-worker of the deceased to see what tributes they bring. He then suggests that you turn this imaginary funeral into your own in order to consider what you would like people to say. This exercise, he argues, will help you adopt one of the secrets of highly effective people in that they live with the end in mind.[3] K. Beckstrom put it well in one sentence, "Live so the preacher can tell

---

[3] Stephen Covey, *The Seven Habits of Highly Effective People* (Simon and Schuster, 1989), 98.

the truth at your funeral."[4]

Jesus of Nazareth was a highly effective individual, and in his finishing moment you can see that he had kept this end in mind throughout his race. Not only did he show acute awareness in the immediate events leading up to this time, but should you look back through his life story, you can see he regularly and frequently foretold these events, demonstrating that he had them in his mind and was constantly preparing for their arrival. So how can you develop this skill and use it to steer you to a good finish? How can you act now to turn all your beginnings into healthy endings? I suggest that if you look back over the previous six hours on this hill, a blue print will come into focus that will equip you to assess how you are doing in this respect.

A MODEL EMERGES

Let me lay it out for you a series of questions that will diagnose your finishing health. As I ask them, you will see that I am basing them on the previous five phrases spoken from this workshop cross, combining them to form a measuring instrument against which you can hold your life and work. Here are the questions:

Have you learned how to pray in the face of stress, deriving your sense of worth, security, and values from the Father?

Have you learned to forgive, dropping the list of grievances and bitterness on a regular basis so that you can approach your finish unhindered by a weight of anger?

Have you learned to encourage and create a climate of good news by

---

[4] Commonly attributed to K. Beckstrom, the original source material is uncertain.

affirming those around you and helping them hear the whispers of paradise?

Have you learned to live life in the moment, doing the right thing at the right time, with a sense of mission and purpose that connects with your ability to handle days well, reduce worry, delegate, and mission, so that there is harmony in your soul?

Have you, when required, stood for what is right and against what is wrong?

Have you learned to express the authentic, best expression of who you are and how you were designed?

Have you revealed need, asked for help, and drawn strength from others?

As you have run, have you really been yourself?

All these questions and more arise out of the five phrases we have heard from the carpenter's cross. The beauty of the story now is that you can see them combining and connecting as you race, helping you head for a healthy finish. And by the way, if you are reading this and thinking that it is rather late for you, then you should jog back to the second saying and remember that the dying thief did not have any time to put these great principles into practice – but he still finished well. The sadness for him was that he could have started his finish much earlier and enjoyed the race for much longer. But the carpenter isn't hamstrung by your late arrival to the party – he's smarter than that.

The thief we met earlier didn't know it, but "It is finished" marked the closing of a cosmic agreement, a mystical moment happening right next to him when the Father God, Son of God, and Spirit of God drew back the curtain and let us glimpse the resolution of what is now called the new covenant. It is almost impossible to find adequate words to describe what is happening here because we are looking at events that go beyond our ability to understand. Some find the descriptions I am using beyond their beliefs, while others have based their whole lives around them. Whatever your stance or understanding, let me invite you to look and learn, because the lessons that emerge will, I promise you, speak directly into your work, your life, your race, and your ability to finish.

THE REAL DEAL

If, as I am proposing here, we have a glimpse of such an agreement, it has to be the ultimate real deal. As we have seen, agreements form the framework for achievement. Therefore, this agreement cannot only give you a model of how to do real deals, but can itself provide the framework for you to achieve the greatest of all achievements – your life.

We all do deals every day, so why not look through this window for a vision of how to do them well? To help me think about this whole area, I spent some time discussing with a very close friend of mine who specializes in doing deals, the hallmarks of a good one. I had studied the carpenter and my friend had studied the market, so we tried to pool our wisdom and do justice to this moment. Following are some of our conclusions.

THE HALLMARKS OF A GOOD DEAL

Good deals must be fair deals. A win-lose deal is always a bad deal because someone walks away disappointed. You already know this because you have experienced both the fair and the unfair. To ask, "Is it fair?" is a powerful indicator in human negotiations of the health of an agreement.

The glimpse we have of this ultimate deal Jesus was making in his final hours is that he was offering the gift of total forgiveness for all failure. It is a free pardon for all who ask for it, an invitation to be brought into the embrace of divine goodness and care. The agreement includes the ongoing support, teaching, and resourcing of a personal presence in your life to empower you to understand, enjoy, and celebrate the new relationship on offer. The price of all of this was paid by the carpenter himself who was, in those six final hours, doing the work he contracted to do – rescuing humanity from self-destruction.

The motivation behind all of this was the desire of the Father to forgive, and his promise to accept the payment in full was his part of the agreement. The third contribution was the one made by the invisible Spirit of God who had committed himself to make this agreement real, present, and effective for racers for centuries to come. And that is why today there are still so many who follow the ways of the carpenter-turned-teacher. It is just a fact you can observe, but the observable outcome is a direct result of this mystical contract creating the framework for long-term, unequalled achievement.

So, is it fair? All I can say is that the terms and conditions seem to go beyond fair into incredibly generous. Those racers who have chosen to accept them have found that they were even more generous than they expected. And this is why, surprise after surprise, they follow the decision to go the way of the carpenter and race with his whispers of paradise in their souls.

While you consider these things, we may now be able to agree that good deals are fair deals, and perhaps pool a bit more wisdom to identify additional best practices in deal making, agreements, and finishing well.

To find a healthy agreement the best negotiators also try very hard to understand the other party's point of view and personal position. This is illustrated in the comments made many years ago by Francis De Sales, who became bishop of Geneva, "Make yourself a seller when you are buying and a buyer when you are selling, and then you will sell and buy justly."[5] The principle was also finely summarized by American author and hotelier Orison Swett Marden, "The golden rule for every business man is this: 'Put yourself in your customer's place.'"[6]

Preceding both of these gentlemen came a comment in our regularly quoted Sermon on the Mount. The comment has been labeled the golden rule: "So in everything, do to others as you would have them do to you."[7]

You can see that business people and thinkers down through the centuries have concurred on the principle of understanding the other party. The question before us is whether or not we find it in the agreement being sealed and delivered on the Jerusalem hill?

THE WORK OF UNDERSTANDING

You don't have to go far back even in those six hours to find your answer. The man who said, "I am thirsty" had tasted the reality of humanity with all its physical intricacies and limitations. The man who said, "My God, my God, why have you forsaken me?" had drank from the bitter cup of human isolation and terror. He was a man who had wrestled with his priorities as he attempted to deal with his life's work

---

[5] Tony Castle, *A Treasury of Christian Wisdom* (Hodder and Stoughton, 2001), 31.

[6] http://en.thinkexist.com/quotation/the_golden_rule_for_every_business_man_is _this-/264387.html

[7] Matthew 7:12

while caring for family and friends. He had experienced the dilemmas you experience daily, if not hourly. He was a man who had given hope and encouragement. He had struggled with stress and had run the gauntlet of human thoughts, emotions, and choices, identifying fully and completely with every temptation, challenge, and enterprise that we all experience. And as he shouted, "It is finished!" he was completing both the agreement and his part in it, as well as his total 33-year journey of identification with those he came to reach.

In short, this agreement was one being hammered out by someone who totally understood you, from stress to celebration, and all highs and lows in between. It was the real deal because it factored in the conditions of real humanity.

So if you are an employee, you need to understand your employer so you can design good agreements and maximize good achievement. If you are a manager, it is vital you understand your reports so you can play to their strengths, cover for their weaknesses, and get the job done right.

This principle applies to every working relationship you develop. If you are a woman, try to understand men so you can do good business with them. If you are a man, work on your understanding of women so you can learn their working languages and unique skills.

As we have seen, this empathetic, altruistic stance is absolutely crucial if you are to buy and sell. What does the other party want? What are they looking for? What would encourage them to choose your product or service or enter into an agreement with you?

Let's be clear here. In this race of rats, you will not always find that you are dealing with racers who share these values of fairness and understanding that I am identifying as hallmarks of good deal making. Many people want to get a win-lose deal where they take as much and concede as little as possible. They want to manipulate whatever micro-market you are in so they can line their pockets, whatever the cost to you.

Herein lies the challenge for you to consider: Will you race the carpenter's way, or the way of the dirty rat? Dirty deals may create short-term successes, but they don't lead to great finishes. They rob all those concerned with dignity and value, creating a grubby marketplace built on shaky foundations. Sooner or later, someone will crack a whip and drive such dealmakers out of their temples to self-worship.

If you want to race with the carpenter, then some deals will be off. He will want to equip you with the skills to play fair, and he'll give you the insight to understand your opposite number so you can start, carry on, achieve, and finish well.

THE MOMENT OF DECISION

Assuming a deal is on, however, notice that you are looking at a decisive moment in this sixth phrase. It was a time when the agreement was actually reached, when the issues were all settled. There comes a time in any negotiation process when the deal is closing. I thought I knew how to do deals until I saw a professional deal-maker in action. Having found fair terms, covered all eventualities, and divided costs and benefits, he stopped dealing. Many a deal is spoiled because a party does not know how to spot the decisive, conclusive moment and close negotiations at that point. A nervous continuation of discussions and questions starts to liquefy a solid deal and cause it to run through your fingers like mercury, resulting in an unnecessary re-negotiation. Good deals may include room for further sub-deals, but the decisive moment in each process is the time to stop, sign, shake hands, and close.

WHAT IF?

But we're not finished yet. According to my deal-maker friend, good agreements cover future possible outcomes by exploring and predicting the inherent risks and making provisions for them. In short, they cover the "what ifs." What if the product can't be delivered on time? What if the price of raw materials dramatically changes? What if a key researcher leaves or a chief executive defects to another company?

These "what ifs" operate when mergers and acquisitions take place, and they are found at the top levels of business. There are numerous "what ifs" that percolate into an individual's work contracts. What if you become ill or injured? What if you become pregnant? What if, for various reasons, you need to take a leave of absence? What if you uncover a fraud?

These issues fall into the area labeled "human resources" and present a massive challenge to companies and businesses, whether there are two or three employees or a multinational workforce of thousands. Good deals mean fair deals, and fair deals cover "what ifs," not just for employees in one area, but globally.

Consider whether your current lifestyle is built on the back of a marketplace in which employees somewhere in the world are working in conditions that you would never accept and in which people are less than human in handling resources. If you are in a position of influence, providing you want to race well, you must face the facts about "what ifs," not just locally and personally, but globally.

Such is the nature of the real deal cemented in the "It is finished" moment. You can capture the built-in covering of eventualities simply by looking at how the moment played out. What if you stumble, fall, or fail? There is help, restoration, and forgiveness built-in. What if you get confused? There is wisdom available. What if you don't know where to turn? There is a written record of the original agreement and verbal testimony of millions of racers to help you see the light. What if you find yourself alone? You will find the carpenter standing next to you.

That is the point of this book. This is not a mere analysis of the rat race, nor is it a self-help psychological handbook. The real deal involves a profound partnership between Jesus and you, the racing rat, resulting in an altogether revolutionized racing style.

GOING GLOBAL

Although personal, this partnership is not a private arrangement for a privileged few. It is designed to spread across the globe, empowering any who want it to find a new way and figure out how to work with humanity and dignity.

This is a slightly grandiose way of saying that all workers should have rights, privileges, and freedoms in a just and fair market, and each of us who has tasted the carpenter's wine should pass the glass around by making sure we do all in our power to give workers around the world the good news that they need and the best practices they deserve. The carpenter on the hill is a generous giver, but he will also ask of us racers, "What if you received the good news and didn't pass it around?" This too is part of the real deal and plays itself out in the working conditions we create as we race our races.

Once you start thinking globally about the fairness and integrity of deal making, it is not a massive mental leap to consider the relationship into which we enter with the environment itself. In today's marketplace, there is an increasing awareness that environmental factors must be considered when doing business. Partly through awareness, partly through fear, and with a growing sense of financial necessity, we are recovering a sense of responsibility when using the world's resources.

AVOIDING WASTE

Perhaps it will help you to remember that this piece of work we are examining, lasting six hours on the Jerusalem hill, was essentially a rescue mission. We have seen the rescue in relation to stress, hope, balance, integrity, and authenticity, and in these closing moments you can legitimately reflect that this mission is not just for individual racers, but for the race itself. The new way of racing you are exploring has far-reaching implications that spread into your view of the environment.

When teaching his learners about handling a large consignment of food, this same carpenter concluded the process with the words, "Let nothing be wasted."[8] It's another small phrase with large lessons and enormous significance. To race well and finish well, to achieve, and to do good deals will include an intentional avoidance of waste. It is the waste of global resources that devalues the human race and creates poor contracts between all of us who are mere visitors renting space for a time and the landlord who owns the space we occupy. Recovering this sense of delegated responsibility will help you to align your personal business lifestyle with the avoidance of waste and the achievement of results.

Of course, this principle applies across all boards of human activity. It is disastrous if talent and gifting is wasted or if time is just thrown away. Precious, valuable commodities are to be found everywhere either by excavating the ground or exploring the mind of the person next to you. Good deal makers won't waste either.

---

8   John 6:12

ANOTHER TOOLKIT

You are now in a position to look straight through the window of this phrase and catch a view of a specific skill set that Jesus of Nazareth demonstrated that you can employ in your life and work. When you look, you will be able to see at least half a dozen skills in the set and I'll spell them out for you.

First, he understood his mission. It is very difficult, if not impossible, to achieve something if you have not obtained and understood your mission. You may achieve something, but if you have misunderstood your mission, you will find yourself running up blind alleys or down side-tracks.

For Jesus of Nazareth to be able to shout "Finished!" with the power and confidence contained in the loudness of his words, he had to have spent many years figuring out his mission. We don't have detailed records of his early years, but we have numerous glimpses and plenty of information from his later years to show us how his life was shaped. At 12 years of age, he was taken from the small town of Nazareth to the big city of Jerusalem for the national Jewish celebration of the beginnings of freedom, called Passover. At the end of the visit, the Nazareth party left and Jesus' parents naturally assumed he was somewhere in the group. On finding out he was not with them, they retraced their steps and found the boy asking astonishing questions of the learned leaders back in Jerusalem. On receiving the understandably exasperated ear-bashing from his parents, his response was that he had to be about his "Father's business."[9]

Here is your glimpse of a boy working on understanding his mission. He was deepening his own awareness of the reasons why he was born.

---

[9] Luke 2:49

Passover was simultaneously a powerful and yet grotesque festival. Hundreds of thousands of animals would have been slaughtered over the days and the results could be seen in the pink water flowing in the urban streams. He knew that his job was to bring an altogether different kind of Passover, hallmarked with a profound quality of freedom that no one had ever seen. Twenty years after this event, he would be in the city again. It would be Passover again, and he would be the victim, not the witness, as he finished his work on the hill outside the walls.

Here we can see a powerful skill for every task. Have you understood your mission? It applied to Jesus as he spent 30 years figuring out his life's mission, and it applies to you and me, because we have to work on finding our major purpose. You have already seen the importance of life purpose as you looked through the other phrases from the cross, but here you can see the value of having an overall sense of mission for your life in order to keep racing with achievement and finishing well.

This skill also applies to the projects, tasks, or jobs you do on a day-to-day basis. How many projects fail because the mission was not clear and not understood? If you or others around you do not know what is expected of you, then the only thing that you can expect is confusion.

DETAILS

The second skill is to give attention to all the details. By age 30, Jesus not only understood his mission, which he articulated in his various mission statements, he had also made a number of specific, strategically detailed decisions. One of the most important decisions was that he chose who he wanted to be in his team to go on a 36-month learning journey that would change them and the world forever. Getting 12 leaders was essential, and among these 12 he had three closer figures named Peter, James, and John; and among these three he had a right-hand man to whom he would eventually entrust his mother. That man was John.[10]

To this team he explained the nature of their shared task as well as the tasks only he could do. He painstakingly involved them at ever deeper levels with his rescue mission and crucially laid out for them what this enterprise would cost. He warned them of the pitfalls and prepared them for the opposition.

This second scoping phase is vital if you want to achieve anything at all. It is the defining of the strategic detail that separates out the successful from the mediocre, and will enable you and others around you to fulfill their missions and deliver the desired results.

The third skill in this set is that of ownership, or responsibility. It is so pleasant to be part of a group or involved with a co-worker who, in the face of a heavy workload, says of specific aspects, "I will do that." It is music to a manager's ears.

Time after time in the profile records of Jesus of Nazareth, which we now call the gospels, you can hear him say, "I am...," "I will...," or "I have come to...," followed by a description of his ownership of tasks and promise of delivery. Elsewhere, he is quoted as saying, "Here I am, I have come to do your will oh God,"[11] which was a perfect summary of his responsibility and ownership. This responsibility and ownership resulted in him finishing his tasks on a hill in full view of Jerusalem's city wall. As a student of history, he would have been aware of a time nearly five centuries before, when another great

---

[10] The record of his team assembly is found in various places, with one example being Mark 3:16

[11] Hebrews 10:7

finisher had organized large numbers of people to re-build the derelict walls in preparation for a return of the refugee population.

The man's name was Nehemiah, and an entire chapter of the book that bears his name is dedicated to recording the names of the workers and the tasks that they did. Each person, it is recorded, took responsibility for a section of the wall, and it took 52 days before they could say "finished." And here is a powerful illustration of ownership. As we previously learned, delegation is an antidote to worry, but there are some things that can't be delegated, because they are your bit of the wall, and finishing it is your responsibility. By the way, the construction manager overseeing the wall project concluded that it had been built with the help of God.[12] What I am suggesting to you is that adopting the skills of the carpenter will enlist the help of God as you build whatever you build.

The fourth skill for your set is to do everything in the required way. In my work, we have a large document called "procedures." It contains tips, advice, and processes, laid out in a detailed fashion, as to how to best perform the tasks we need to carry out to run our work. They are regularly revised as we discover better ways to do various projects or when new technologies or tasks are added. Currently, they are the best expression of how we should operate. I have had staff members who have used the procedures to serve our purposes and do things in the required way, and then I also have had other staff whose entire mission seemed to be to rewrite the procedures before even learning and applying them. If you are a manager, you know how frustrating it can be if a staff member insists on doing things in an inappropriate way. I'm not talking about creativity or useful initiative, but stubborn non-cooperation.

---

[12] Nehemiah 6:16

Jesus of Nazareth made it his aim to do things well and to do them in the right way. So he explained that it mattered to him, not only what he said, but how he said it.[13] He refused to give in to the temptation to take shortcuts or become inauthentic, because that was not the right way to do things.

There is a bumper sticker that reads, "Please be patient, because God isn't finished with me yet." The intriguing thing is that, as you attempt to work the carpenter's way, you will discover that God is working on you, helping you to grow into the finished piece of work, while you try to finish your tasks.[14] Finishing is about what you do, how you do it, and what you become as you do it.

To introduce the fifth skill of the set, I ask you to call to mind a phrase that is often used as a resigned statement of frustration, or occasionally despondency. In the face of a particularly testing time, people often say, "Well, we all have our crosses to bear." It is a phrase that has its origin in a statement recorded for us by a medical practitioner, named Luke, who knew a few things about burdens that people had to carry. Luke's record of Jesus' words reads, "Take up your cross daily and follow me."[15] You have seen throughout this book that taking up of the cross means many things in relation to handling stress or living a balanced life, but in this finishing phrase, I suggest to you that it can be enlisted to help you think about what you should finish on a daily basis. It includes, but is not exclusively related to, a daily to-do list, because it goes beyond immediate tasks to such issues as what project, conversation, conflict, or misunderstanding we should resolve in a particular day. This kind of thinking will enable you to at least assess your daily progress but, perhaps more importantly, it will enable you

---

[13] John 12:49

[14] James 1:6

[15] Luke 9:23

to learn what it means to finish a day well. American poet Ralph Waldo Emerson advised, "Finish each day before you begin the next, and interpose a solid wall of sleep between the two."[16] Considering what you are being called to finish each day will help you achieve and even celebrate on a daily basis the progress of your race.

Your sixth skill is to be found in the fact that this expression, "It is finished," comes to us not in a tentative or timid voice, but in a loud shout. It is meant to be heard. The thieves hanging beside him, the small group with John and Mary, the Roman guards surrounding the execution site, and all spectators to these mysterious moments heard a resounding report that the job was done.

How often have you been frustrated by asking if a task has been done, only to discover that it has been completed, but no one told you? The result of such secrecy is that you have to retain some responsibility in your head and cannot let go of the connection to that task in the knowledge that it is completed.

No such secrecy existed here on this day as you are listening to the ultimate report spoken with complete clarity, in no uncertain terms, by a man confident that he has finished the work he was commissioned to do.

So in your skill set, make sure that when you have taken the mission, scoped the detailed strategy, taken responsibility, done all things in the required way, and carried your daily cross, that you clearly and completely report to the relevant people that the work has indeed been done. It is an extremely refreshing habit for all concerned, as it presents another opportunity to celebrate and move healthily on.

---

[16] http://en.thinkexist.com/quotation/finish_each_day_before_you_begin_the_next-and/262354.html

TEMPORARY VS. PERMANENT

There are so many simultaneous finishes occurring in this moment on the hill that you could be forgiven for feeling bombarded with ideas. I did warn you that they may merge, but even though the moment is concentrated, it contains so many rich rewards that it is worth holding on until we have found as many as we can.

One such reward can be obtained if you think again about the Passover festival to which I referred earlier. It was a part of a whole series of events and spiritual expressions designed to form a framework for life, work, and civilized living. It included a variety of rituals and beautiful symbolic activities that still have a dignity and attraction today. But much of that system was always meant to be temporary. It was put in place pending the arrival of a complete, deeper, more effective, and permanent order that would create the capacity for radical human rescue and personal renewal. When the carpenter shouted, "It is finished," he was signaling that this was the end of the old ways and the ushering in of a new and best quality order containing powerful and elegant solutions to the conundrums that humanity was facing.

This is what we are watching being played out during this six-hour drama – a way to pray to the Father, a way of forgiveness, a way to paradise, a way to balance, a way to integrity, and a way to live, work, and die. Simultaneously, it was the end of the old ways along with the arrival of the best way. In fact, just a few hundred yards from where he shouted, the massive curtain in the Jerusalem temple he had visited just a week earlier, ripped from top to bottom in another mystical moment of high drama full of clear signals that things had radically changed. This curtain had symbolically separated God from common people, and now it had been torn apart by the finishing act of Jesus, representing a foundational shift in the way things would work from there on out.

As you race, you can take this thinking with you, recognizing that temporary arrangements are by definition temporary, and if they are left in place too long, they lead to discouragement and low morale. Many is the high school that has erected temporary classrooms and used them for far too many years to the detriment of the education of the students and the well-being of the teaching staff. When temporary contracts are left in place for too long they can create uncertainty and fear in the minds of workers who never know when the axe will fall. Good racers know that such arrangements need to be finished and simultaneously replaced with the best order.

A strange paradox has been associated with some spiritual approaches to work in the belief that they combine high spiritual mindedness with low professional standards. The carpenter's way of racing is the best way, not only because it works, but because it works well to a high level of quality. Spectators to Jesus' working practices came to a clear conclusion as they remarked, "He has done everything well."[17]

Let me gently encourage you to remember this on a daily basis when you go into the marketplace. The ways of the carpenter are not just for family life, church life, or charitable causes; they are not just about private morality applied to a few key issues. The carpenter's ways represent a new way of working, in which the old curses of stress, inauthenticity, discouragement, drudgery, and the devaluing of human dignity and balance are gone, and if you want to race with him, he wants to show you a new way of racing and a new way of being the best. "It's not true that nice guys finish last," according to Addison Walker. "Nice guys are winners before the game even starts."[18]

---

[17] Mark 7:37

[18] http://en.thinkexist.com/quotation/it-s_not_true_that_nice_guys_finish_last-nice/10084.html

RETIRED? DISCHARGED?

While we are reflecting on finishes, some racers reading these words may have retired from paid work and be wondering how to view the last laps of the race. If that's you and you haven't finally decided to buy your home in Florida, take up sky-diving, or learn to knit dog clothing, you should consider that, for Jesus of Nazareth, his life and his life's work ended simultaneously. He saw his task as completing the work he had been commissioned to do by his father. If you race with him, this will also be true of you. Of course, this is good news if you are an activist, but not such good news if you are a beach addict. Richard Bach, author of *Jonathan Livingston Seagull*, put it like this, "Here is the test to find if your mission on earth is finished: If you're alive, it isn't."[19]

This is an important component in making sure you know you are valued, needed, and significant, whatever your age. There is wisdom, experience, and power in your soul that means the race is not over until you've finally finished. Some extremely busy retirees know this, but many find that there is a feeling of being superfluous, irrelevant, or past the sell-by date associated with finishing a career path. This is not how the carpenter sees you, for he invites you to explore with him the authentic expression of who you are in every era of your life, including the last one, until you are then invited, along with the thief, to walk in a walled garden at an altogether different pace.

Finally in this survey of finishes, it is a significant truth to understand that this was an ending with a beginning. When, as we will see, he finally breathed his last, he was finished, but other things were starting. If you want evidence, just hold this book up in the air for a moment,

---

[19] Richard Bach, *Jonathan Livingston Seagull* (HarperCollins Publishers Ltd; New edition 22 Aug 1994).

because it is a physical expression of the fact that he started us thinking about how to race. Drive in most neighborhoods and it won't be very long until you see a cross, a place of worship, or a hospital built in his name. Look through the pages of history, or into your own soul and you will see what started when he said "finished." This rat race is a relay race, and if you run this way you will pass the baton to younger racers who will outlive you and carry your legacy to further finishes long after you are gone.

This chapter is now finished.

LAP SEVEN: SPIRITUAL NOURISHMENT – THE GRASS BY THE WATER

Every day when you go to work, running a few more steps of your race, you carry deep within you something that is beyond you, and yet it is part of you. It is a striving or longing so buried in your being that it resides in the hidden places, and yet it is found everywhere. It is a part of you that yearns for work to mean something, for your life to matter, and for your contribution to count. It is a desire to find a satisfying answer to an often unspoken but ever-present question that drifts discreetly through your mind, "Isn't there more to life than this?"

Each of us seems to be born with a congenital dissatisfaction with the tangible world, a kind of suspicion that all is not as it seems, connected to a developing disbelief in the information before our own eyes. You can see this dissatisfaction played out in a hundred dramas, a thousand thoughts, and a million moments. Look up at a night sky, and even if you have some training in astronomy, you wonder what or who lies beyond. Witness the birth of a child, and even if you have studied physiology, you cannot cope with the cascade of emotions moving you to awe. Watch two people in love, and you know you can't bottle the force that is far greater than either individual or both of them combined. Even in the face of absurdity, you look for things to make sense, and even in the depths of despair, you want to find hope. Trapped, though you are, in time and timetables, you have a constant nagging feeling that there is a dimension beyond time, a world above space and a life after death.

This, I suggest to you, is a thumbnail sketch of the human spirit. It is a universal hunger and thirst that will not be met or quenched with conventional produce, but continues to hunt for invisible nourishment. In your spirit, there is an almost irrational belief that the grass is greener in some as-yet-undiscovered field that is irrigated by pure, crystal-clear streams. In short, you are looking for spiritual nourishment that you suspect will only be found in this grass by the water.

THE RIDDLE OF THE SPIRIT

I hope you love your work and find great pleasure in doing what you do every day. I hope you are fairly paid, honorably treated, and progressing well. As you race, you will perhaps climb up steep hills and may even reach the top of your chosen profession, business, or trade. The pleasures associated with such progress are enormous; you may even fulfill a few dreams and achieve lifelong ambitions along the way. No matter how successful, wealthy, or fulfilled you are, you know that the needs of your spirit cannot be met at the deepest level by such successes. This is not to write them off, because money, power, achievement, status, education, progress, and recognition are all massive motivators and essential for your wellbeing. It's just that, on their own, they can't solve the riddle of your spirit. The irony is that, the more fulfilled you are on a day-to-day basis, the more you can ignore your spirit or pretend the puzzle has gone away. But as you reach your closing laps, the question becomes more pressing, more persistent, and echoes more loudly in your brain. As you face your last moments, the issue of your spirit comes into sharpest focus, because it is then that your race straddles the boundary between the now and the beyond, causing you to wonder if your wheeling, dealing, and racing has purchased you a passport to oblivion or paradise.

It's fitting then, that we now come to that same boundary, between the now and beyond, in the carpenter's race. It is here that we will learn how to solve the puzzle of the spirit. Here is where his last words from the cross will give you your seventh window and complete the set of skills that we have been gathering from Jesus for the racing rat. It is Luke, the doctor, who recorded these words for us in his carefully researched account:

"Jesus called out in a loud voice, 'Father, into your hands I commit my spirit!'"[1]

While we leave these words hanging in the air for a moment, let's be clear about what we are trying to achieve by taking a good, long look at spirituality. I am suggesting to you that the race you are running – the work you do day by day – will be infinitely more rewarding, satisfying, and meaningful if you run with a nourished spirit. I am not advocating that some spiritual activity be added to your work as an optional extra or some bolt-on accessory. I am saying that you are a spiritual being, and that work is also a spiritual activity. Ben and Jerry's co-founder, Jerry Greenfield, observed, "We added value to the company by doing business the way we did it. There is a spiritual aspect to business."[2]

The earlier in your race that you solve this puzzle of the spiritual, the sooner you will benefit from the energy of fulfillment that it brings, and then your entire race will be revolutionized. As you probably have realized already, the whole of this book and all of the previous six sayings from the Jerusalem hill are combined to contribute to the solution of the spiritual puzzle. All of the skills advocated so far have been aimed at the whole of you, using an integrated strategy consisting of caring for your body, renewing your mind, releasing your emotions, rescuing your soul, and nourishing your spirit. But this seventh saying from the carpenter is specifically relevant to the dynamic of staying spiritually nourished, alert, and healthy while you are busy – not in the gaps or quieter moments, but all the time, every day, and in whatever you are doing.

---

[1]   Luke 23:46

[2]   http://en.thinkexist.com/quotation/we-added-value-to-the-company-by-doing-business/567641.html

ATTEMPTED SOLUTIONS

In order to progress on your road to spirituality, you will find it helpful to reflect on the ways that we humans have attempted to solve this riddle or puzzle or spirituality. Of course, some assert that the whole issue is an illusion. According to them, your body is all that there is, your life is the one shot you get, and when you finish, it's over. They say that, in this universe, there is a godless heaven looking down on a soulless earth with a lifeless past, an ultimately meaningless present, and a hopeless future. The only certainty that anyone can offer a baby as they raise her up from the cradle is that someone will one day lower her into a grave.

Although the picture I paint of this landscape is very bleak, it is accurate and logical. Of course, those who hold such a view don't automatically plunge themselves into despair, for part of the deal in living with such views is that individuals look for short-term, immediate meaning and purpose, often identifying certain activities as worthwhile. So they focus on matters of relationships, family, and leaving some sort of lasting legacy. But the fact remains that, if there is nothing beyond the visible or the grave, there is also no ultimate meaning or hope. The past is really gone, the present remains somewhat absurd, and there is no long-term future. When you're done, you're done. No one who holds such view denies the search for meaning and satisfaction, for that is plain to see. Rather, they assert that believing in the mystical is a mistake and the puzzle is only solved if you let go of the idea of spirituality altogether.

Considering the fact that you have reached the seventh lap of your race, I am assuming that the perspective described above is not your preferred approach. But in the real world of work, you will rub shoulders with numerous individuals who hold such views, and it will help you work with them more effectively if you carry with you as you race an understanding and an analysis of their thinking. You may even have a desire to dialogue with them in order to encourage them to re-think, in which case our continued survey of spirituality will help you see further steps along the way and identify other approaches to solving the puzzle.

HUMAN SPIRITUALITY

In the marketplace today, there is increasing talk of a concept called "spiritual intelligence." Here is a description taken from the cover of a book with that same title:

Today's western culture is characterized by selfishness, materialism, a lack of morals, lack of values, lack of a sense of community, and ultimately a lack of meaning. Yet common values, customs, purposes, and meanings are what bind a community together. If society isn't providing these anchors, the answer is to develop individuals' SQ (spiritual intelligence quota) and find your own. SQ is intelligence with which we balance meaning and value, and place our lives in a wider context. It is the 'ultimate intelligence,' as without it both EQ (emotional intelligence quota) and IQ (intellectual intelligence quota) cannot function – they crumble away.[3]

Abraham Maslow, originator of the famous hierarchy of needs concept, in which he identified different levels of human need, ranging from basic survival through total luxury, has become universally quoted in psychology classes. In relation to spirituality, he somewhat complicatedly observed:

"Without the transcendent and transpersonal, we get sick, violent, and

---

[3] Danah Zohar and Ian Marshall, *Spiritual Intelligence: The Ultimate Intelligence* (Bloomsbury, 2000).

nihilistic, or else hopeless and apathetic. We need something 'bigger than we are'... to be awed by and to commit ourselves to in a new, naturalistic, empirical, non-churchly sense."[4]

Some neuroscientists are actively searching for the "God spot" in the brain – a specific area that fires up during prayer, worship, or meditation.

What all these individuals or schools of thought are identifying is the universal human spirituality that expresses itself in countless activities designed to solve the puzzle and end the search. It is an attempt to connect with or harness the power of unseen energy. And this is not only found in massage spas or specialist retreat centers. In fact, many corporate training companies factor human spirituality concepts into their learning programs, and the business world is not averse to exploring such ways to improve results in the bottom line by letting people lift their eyes to a top line. Strategically, this makes perfect sense, for modern workers will surely work better if their deeply held values and beliefs are enlisted as allies, rather than treated as intruders in the marketplace. Values-driven people will drive values into the financial profits of a company much more effectively if they are liberated to be authentic in their work.

William James defined religion as, "The attempt to be in harmony with the unseen order of things." M. Scott Peck observed that today we would tend to see such words as an accurate description of human *spirituality* rather than religion.[5] What the marketplace is slowly

---

[4] Abraham H. Maslow, *Toward a Psychology of Being*, 2nd edition (New York: Van Nostrand Reinhold Company, 1968), 206.

[5] M. Scott Peck, *Further Along the Road Less Traveled: The Unending Journey Toward Spiritual Growth* (New York: Simon & Schuster, 1993), 233. Peck is quoting William James, *The Varieties of Religious Experience* (New York: Modern Library, 1902).

discovering is that the harmony and order contained in James' words can be harnessed for business purposes.

RELIGIOUS SPIRITUALITY

When spirituality starts to get organized, we tend to give it the label "religion." Kenneth Pargament, professor of psychology of religion at Bowling Green University, defined religious spirituality as "the search for significance in ways related to the sacred."[6] So now spirituality becomes connected to sacred days, times, places, or activities. Certain behaviors become sacred along with specific individuals.

Of particular relevance to our race is the idea that certain types of work have been labeled sacred and associated with churches, priests, monasteries, monks, or nuns. In the field of religious spirituality, some people are seen as doing sacred work, while others, probably the majority, are seen as doing secular work. The personal, religious beliefs of a worker are not the determining factor here; rather, it is the work itself that has become defined as secular, whoever is doing it.

So, unfortunately, deal making, business activity, buying and selling, financial services, attorneys, realtors, or builders all are seen to be in the secular world of work. Of course, some doctors, nurses, and teachers almost qualify for sacred status and may get more mentions at church prayer gatherings.

Furthermore, some individuals with deeply held religious beliefs will openly express a longing to cross over from the secular to the sacred as they wait for a "higher calling" that will give them permission to

---

[6] Kenneth I. Pargament, *The Psychology of Religion and Coping* (The Guilford Press, 1997), 32.

relinquish their roles in the marketplace, exchanging customer orders for holy orders carried out in the vestry rather than industry.

This dangerous divide has left the majority of workers in the marketplace devalued, de-motivated, and relegated to the position of second-class citizens. It has falsely labeled some career paths as pilgrimages and others as just regular roads to be taken by ordinary people, marking time until retirement, ordination, or death raises them from their mundane existence to some higher level of operating. This thinking has promoted a subliminal level of guilt that many hold because they love their work. They get a great buzz from success, enjoy making money, or derive deep pleasure from the outcomes they produce, while deep down they feel they are not supposed to enjoy such "secular," meaningless activity.

Far from nourishing the spirit, this sacred-secular divide has starved it. This has left many racers, who thought they had found the grass by the water, struggling to run, gasping for air, and plagued by unnecessary pain. Even those who want to remember their spiritual lives tend to forget their connectedness and are reduced to finding refreshment by taking small sips of encouragement at Sunday services or the occasional conference.

THE CARPENTER'S SOLUTION

There is another way to solve the puzzle that doesn't involve belief in delusions of the humanist, the vagueness of general spirituality, or the divide of religious labeling. I'm talking about the carpenter's way, and to find it you will need to come back to the seventh saying from the six hours outside Jerusalem. Here's that phrase again:

"Jesus called out in a loud voice, 'Father, into your hands I commit my spirit!'"[7]

This sentence straight away presents you with three massive statements about the spiritual. First, by addressing the words to the Father, it repeats an important theme in the carpenter's race: There is, in fact, a Father to be prayed to, lived for, and worked for. Second, in using the words, "my spirit," Jesus was asserting the reality over illusion of the existence of the spiritual. And third, this sentence describes an intriguing dynamic whereby a spirit can be committed into the hands of the Father.

Remember, this is all taking place within the context of his work, because the cross is his workshop and these words are its windows through which we can see Jesus' racing secrets. So here is the exciting prospect before you: Could it be possible to work in such a way that your spirit is constantly nourished, your work is completely sacred, and you stay connected to the unseen hands that hold your race on a healthy and powerful course?

To turn this exciting prospect into living reality, turn your attention back to the carpenter's prayer. It is not quite what it seems; for it is also a quotation from the Jewish hymn book we call the book of Psalms. It was a prayer that Jewish mothers used to teach their children to pray as they went to bed, and it is a great prayer to have on your lips as you close your eyes. It's no surprise, then, that Jesus had this prayer on his lips as he closed his eyes for the last time.

But there is another twist in the race at the very last moment, because the original version of the prayer said, "Into your hands I commit my

---

7   Luke 23:46

spirit."[8] Jesus deliberately added "Father" to the prayer, and in so doing let you see right to the center of all that has happened to this point. If you want a summary, a perfect picture of the carpenter's mission in general and his solution to the puzzle of the spirit in particular, it is found in this clear, concise prayer.

He came to add "Father" to everything. This is the top-down spirituality of Jesus' life's work. It's a time when timelessness breaks through the mist. When your hand reaching up meet hands reaching down. When you discover, in your longing, that you are longed for. When, in your quest to find, you realize that you have been found. It has been said of such insight that it is to discover that the game of life is poker, not solitaire. In other words, there is someone on the other side of the table.

This is not just mystical, esoteric language designed to exclude rational, hard working people from grasping the point; this is the means by which your entire working life can be transformed. If you stay with me in this grass by the water, you will discover a supply of spiritual nourishment that will fuel your whole race.

ADDING CHANGES EVERYTHING

So what does it mean to add "Father" to everything? First, it means that prayer is a way of life. Remember Jesus' first phrase six hours ago, "Father, forgive them...." That phrase served as a window through which you looked and discovered that the Father prayer is a default reaction to stress and pressure, a reaction that was perfectly demonstrated to you by Jesus at work. This default reaction was not cultivated in that moment; it was embedded in and demonstrated

---

[8] Psalm 31:5

throughout his entire life. So he taught his team, "When you pray, say, 'Father.'"[9] He identified himself as on a mission from his Father, and he was quoted by John as speaking about his Father 45 times in the hours leading up to his arrest.[10] Like every good teacher, he repeated his key points endlessly to solidify the learning in their liquid memories.

Now what I am arguing here is that, if you let the carpenter connect you to the Father, you will not only learn to pray, *but your whole life will become a prayer*. This reveals the absurdity of dividing sacred from secular. True spirituality sees every activity as an act of prayer.

Let me expand and illustrate this for you. One of Jesus' most traveled and articulate early followers, Saul of Tarsus, who became known as Saint Paul after a dramatic encounter with the carpenter that revolutionized his race, described being a follower as putting your life on an altar, an activity that he described as reasonable service or spiritual worship.[11]

Yet again we are facing the false divide. In today's world, we tend to see service as some particular form of altruistic work undertaken by well meaning, committed followers of a specific not-for-profit cause. Alternatively, we equate service with holding a public office, or being part of a recognizable type of sector such as financial services or legal services.

Meanwhile, worship is seen as an activity restricted to the devout as they gather in a sacred building to sing songs, say words, and read ancient texts.

---

9   Matthew 6:6-13

10   The account of these hours can be found in John 12-17

11   Romans 12:1

What St Paul was saying, and what Jesus was demonstrating, however, is that *all* work is service, *all* activity is worship, and your whole life is the prayer, the offering, and the expression of your spirituality.

So if you catalogue your daily activities in your mind right now, you might have, for example, making a phone call. With that, I would say every phone call you make is an act of prayer, a reasonable service, or a spiritual service. You may design plans, and I would say that every plan you design is an act of prayer or worship. Your list might include meetings, fixing computers, producing reports, raising invoices, making deals, or helping patients. When you look at your to-do or done list, turn them all into acts of prayer, and you will let the carpenter add Father to your work. Now your work becomes a prayer, and your spirit is starting to be nourished.

Additionally, if you run like this, you will be able to hear whispers of paradise everywhere. Far from forgetting your spirit, you will spot opportunities to remember it all the time. Just before those six hours on the workshop cross, Jesus gathered his team for a final meal. In it, he twisted bread in his hands and passed pieces to his friends. He then poured out some wine and passed around the goblet. Ever the wise teacher, he was giving them a powerful visual aid. He was explaining to them that, when they eat and drink like this, they should remember him. Just hours later, his body would be twisted and broken, his blood poured out, and he wanted them never to forget. So he associated the ordinary act of eating and drinking with the extraordinary acts of his own life's work.

Psychologists sometimes call this "cueing." Another example of cueing would be when cardiac patients are encouraged to wear heart-shaped badges on their clothes to remind them to take care of their hearts that day.

So now you can practice cueing each day by associating the seen with

196

the unseen. When your phone rings, try waiting one more ring, and use that moment to briefly pray for the conversation you are about to have. As you speed dial, pray for the person you are calling. Set your screensaver to flash up words like, "peace," or, "do not worry," to remind you that your Father knows what you need. Let a light switch remind you that Jesus is the light of the world. If you work outdoors, watch the seasons to find opportunities to reflect on the reliability of the Father. The possibilities are endless, but it is very important you don't let the simplicity of the discipline divert you from taking it seriously. You're not learning to put on a bishop's uniform and walk off into the horizon; you are aiming to stay where you are and let the spiritual horizon come to you.

In the seventeenth century, a monk by the name of Brother Lawrence called this type of thinking, "Practicing of the presence of God."[12] It is learning to converse with God all the time, to abandon yourself to Him all the time, constantly watching for moments when the soul can interface with Him. Brother Lawrence spoke of feeding ourselves on Him all the time. It is this constant and consistent mind-set that results in the discovery of nourishment for your spirit and deepens your satisfaction with what you do day by day.

SECURITY AND TRUST

There are, of course, powerful forces at work in the marketplace that will infiltrate your thinking and disturb your peace. One of the greatest of these forces is insecurity. In times of crisis or crunch, you hear nervous talk of job insecurity, financial downturns, and volatile conditions. So this prayer is also an act of deliberate placement of all that you are into

---

[12] Brother Lawrence Hodder, E.M. Blaiklock, trans., *The Practice of the Presence of God* (Stoughton 1987).

the hands of the Father. If you know children, notice that, if you hold something in your hand and playfully challenge them to swipe it away from you, there is nothing they can do unless you let them. The imagery in Jesus' "commit my spirit" prayer is of placing yourself into the strong, secure, and invincible hands of the Father, knowing that no force can swipe you away.

If you want to know what it is like to be in the hands of the Father, just look at the central themes of the carpenter's work. It's about forgiveness, hope, balance, authenticity, and achievement. It also provides no guarantee of an easy race. There is pain, struggle, and hardship, but it is secure. You can lose your job, your comfort, and your company, but you cannot lose your ultimate security, and you should know that your long-term future is therefore resolved.

This perspective allows you to realize that your life is not in the hands of an employer, a manager, or a mortgage company. If you allow the carpenter to add Father to your career, you will also be able to situate yourself in the strong hands of that Father and race with a deep sense of security, even in the face of struggle.

PETER'S PRINCIPLE

It was with struggle in mind that another follower of the carpenter's way – the sword-wielding, hot-headed fisherman called Peter – wrote to a group of workers, telling them that they should bear up under the pain of unjust suffering because they were "conscious of God."[13]

What I have in mind is to keep encouraging you while you work to employ a whole variety of tactics that will help you retain that "God

---

[13]   1 Peter 2:19

consciousness" during your busy times, not just the quiet ones.

The tactics with the telephone or the screen saver that I described earlier as cueing, all form part of your repertoire for keeping your focus and finding your spiritual food. Having said that, you also should consider a couple of disciplines that are not exclusively practiced at work but that I and countless others have found to be helpful in staying conscious of God.

The first is journaling. By this I mean writing down thoughts, ideas, and descriptions of your life as you go along. You may journal once a month or once a day, but if you develop a habit of recording some aspects of your race, you will find that there can be real benefits to this practice. You could, for example, see how issues that were worrying you resolved and what lessons you learned. You could use your journaling to let you see your repeated patterns in relation to stress. You may even allow your written words to form into prayer as you write.

The important thing is to make sure you don't feel guilty if you leave a gap between writing. It is important to not associate guilt with any of the disciplines or tactics described here, because they are meant to be nourishing. In addition, you would be wise to remember that you are not writing for anyone else, so feel free to let your thoughts guide you. I am not saying that journaling or any other disciplines come directly out of the seventh sentence from the cross, but they are logical responses to the needs and drives you have to nourish your spirit and stay conscious of God.

There is another discipline worth mentioning here. Ironically, although nourishing, it involves denial of nourishment. I am referring to fasting. Quite simply, fasting is abstention from food for a higher purpose. Rarely and only for short periods do people abstain from fluids as well, but generally speaking, it applies to food. Whole books have been written on this discipline, but please allow me to make a few comments in passing and refer you to the books if you want to pursue it.[14]

Fasting is a totally biblical practice and was undertaken regularly by many of the key characters in ancient times, as well as the followers of the carpenter's way. Somehow, abstention from food revealed clarity on issues of the spirit and enabled the faster to focus on God. The time frames for fasting have ranged from missing one meal to going without food for 40 days, and all stages in between. (If you want to embark on a longer fast, it is essential to educate yourself, prepare thoroughly, and get medical supervision.) The experiences recorded range from a deep awareness of God's presence to a major sense of struggle, and all shades of emotions and feelings in between – including hunger!

Done responsibly and wisely, fasting can become a health-giving discipline that will help you practice the presence of God. It can be done while you work, although you will need to slow your pace. The key rule is to learn, research, and read about how to fast, especially if you are going to do anything longer than three days. The fruit of fasting can be a renewed awareness of the spiritual nature of life and the learning of some profound lessons about yourself and your journey.

As we draw this line of thinking together, you can see the same ideas being expressed by Peter, Paul, and Brother Lawrence all echo the carpenter's solution to the puzzle of the spirit.

It is important to make some clear distinctions here. It is not the presence of the Father that is in question; it is learning to find ways to practice his presence. Remember, it is not the nature of the work that defines it as sacred, but whether it is laid down on an altar and offered

---

[14] See: Arthur Wallace, *God's Chosen Fast* (Christian Literature Crusade, June 1986). Also see: Joel Fuhrman, *Fasting and Eating for Health* (St Martin's Griffin, 1995).

up as a prayer. And it is not the reality of the Father that is in doubt, but your choice to stay conscious of Him, whatever you do.

The surprise of the carpenter's spirituality is that, as you follow his ways, you discover that the invisible Spirit of God actually works inside of you as an inner teacher, counselor, and guide. Day by day, in the actual tasks you do, the Spirit actively nourishes your spirit with encouraging words when you are nervous, strengthening words when you are tired and comforting words when you are hurting.

Also consider that the vocabulary of words used in your inner space will often be drawn from the written words documented by previous racers – in the record known as the Bible. Jesus chose to call to mind a deliberate quote from one of his Jewish ancestors and bring it out when he needed it most. One of the ways that the boy from Nazareth learned this skill was from his own remarkable mother, who at that moment was standing very close to him as he spoke. It was said of Mary that she hid things in her heart.[15] Here she watched her son bringing out from his heart, for just this moment, an ancient prayer he had hidden for many years. It was a prayer that she may well have prayed with him when he closed his eyes as a young boy at the end of a day.

So here is another solution for the puzzle of the spirit for you to use to stay nourished when you are busy. Why not spend some time hiding ancient wisdom in your heart so that when you need it, it is there? Hide any or all of the seven phrases from the cross, but especially the prayers, in your soul. So when you are stressed, you can pray, "Father, forgive them." Or when you have a hard day to face, you can pray, "Into your hands I commit my spirit."

---

[15] Luke 2:19

WRITE YOUR OWN PSALM

In keeping with Jesus' style of collecting help from the ancient hymn book, you may like to hide David's famous 23rd psalm in your heart. I have a suggestion that will help you get the most out of that psalm. First, learn the original version and hide the six short verses in your heart so you will be ready to bring out when you need them most during work. Here is the psalm for you:

Psalm 23
A psalm of David.
1 The LORD is my shepherd; I shall not be in want.
2 He makes me lie down in green pastures,
he leads me beside quiet waters,
3 he restores my soul.
He guides me in paths of righteousness
for his name's sake.
4 Even though I walk
through the valley of the shadow of death,
I will fear no evil,
for you are with me;
your rod and your staff,
they comfort me.
5 You prepare a table before me
in the presence of my enemies.
You anoint my head with oil;
my cup overflows.
6 Surely goodness and love will follow me
all the days of my life,
and I will dwell in the house of the LORD
forever.

Now take another look at the psalm that begins, "The Lord is my shepherd," and ask yourself what David did for a living. He was a shepherd. Look further down the psalm, and it talks of meals on a battle field. David was also a soldier. So you can see that this shepherd-turned-soldier took both of his own job titles and offered them as descriptions of his Lord. Out of his own inside knowledge of shepherding and military work, he proceeds to write a job description containing detailed clauses, imagining how God would fulfill the role of a perfect shepherd and soldier. There is the power of the psalm – it's a workplace masterpiece. My suggestion to you is that you take your own job title and start off...

"The Lord is my...."

Now place your job title at the end of that first line and then write your own personal "Psalm 23" that details how the Lord would treat you if he were your, for example, accountant, lawyer, teacher, builder, or engineer. Just make sure you put your own job title into the first line. You can then use your inside knowledge of your own job to write your psalm and raise your consciousness of God in your work to a new level.

SLEEPING SPIRITUALLY?

While we're on the subject of consciousness, consider the fact that, for about one-third of your race, you are unconscious, or at least semi-conscious. In other words, you are asleep. Remember that this final prayer was used by Jewish mothers as a bedtime prayer for their children. Many is the exhausted racing rat who arrives at the end of another day's racing only to find that rest and sleep don't always arrive easily. Anxieties and worries from the waking hours spill over into the sleeping hours and rob you of meaningful rest. Is it possible to become conscious of God when you sleep?

If you have raced with me through this entire book, you will remember that the insight for the book came to me one midsummer night in a dream. I became conscious of God as I slept, and I have attempted to share that consciousness with you in these pages. Ironically, I am not a good sleeper, and I rarely awake having had a great night's sleep. I am one of those racers whose mind keeps racing long after my body has stopped. So maybe this prayer can become a window in defining a better way of resting as well as racing. Our old friend David wrote in the fourth psalm:

When you are on your beds,
search your hearts
and be silent.
Offer right sacrifices
and trust in the Lord.[16]

These words contain very similar ideas to the spiritual puzzle solutions we have outlined. You can see the four suggestions in David's poem and you may find them valuable when you toss and turn in sleepless hours after your next difficult day.

THE GIFT

By now, you may be able to see that spirituality is directional. I can best illustrate this by asking you to consider how a young child behaves just after he or she has been given a fantastic birthday present. They give their whole attention to the gift. It absorbs their time. They look at it, taste it, smell it, and hold it. They will neither let it go nor let it out of their sight. They will even take it to bed with them.

Similarly, spirituality is characterized by the object of its attention. You are not a person with a little spirit lodged somewhere in your left leg

---

[16] Psalm 4:4-5

or right brain. You are a spiritual person, and when everything you are – heart, mind, soul, and body – is focused on a particular object, that defines your spirituality.

In this chapter, I have tried to help you find the shepherd of Psalm 23 and let him make you lie down in the green grass beside the quiet waters so you will be radically nourished while you race.

And in this book, I have tried to help you give your entire attention to the amazing gift of the carpenter from Nazareth as he displayed his masterful skills on the surprising workshop cross for six hours on a Jerusalem hill. You have heard him pray and forgive while handling pressure and stress. You have looked over the shoulders of the thief and heard the whisper of paradise and seen the power of hope. You have stood with John and Mary and watched his multi-layered ability to live in the moment, doing the right thing at the right time. You have stood in the darkness and heard him stand alone with integrity in the face of isolation. You have seen them offer him a drink in the time of raw physicality, when his complex humanity expressed itself in authenticity. You have heard him seal the real deal and finish what he set out to do in perfect completion. Now you have heard him breathe his last and solve the spiritual puzzle with exquisite expertise.

If you have raced with me all this way, I hope I have been able to show you how a man who changed the world can change the way you work. And as we run together for a few more paces, I invite you to come and stand with me by one of the closest eyewitnesses to these extraordinary hours and look at the same view that he saw. We don't know his name, only his job title – centurion – and his job was to guard the site. When he saw all that had happened, he said, "Surely, this man was the Son of God."[17]

---

[17] Matthew 27:54

I don't know your name or your job title, but if you are beginning to see what I saw and you are beginning to react as the centurion reacted, then for now, I have done my job and guarded the site of Jesus and the racing rat.

Race well.

COOL DOWN:
METASKILLS –
PERFECTING THE WHOLE

I have been inviting you to stand very close to events that took place many years ago and examine their meaning in detail. As you have done that with me, you have been acquiring sets of skills, collections of insights, and I hope, thousands of tips for you to take into your race. Now I want to ask you to stand back and look at the landscape from farther away. You and I have the benefits of two thousand years of history through which to look at these startling events, along with testimonies of billions of racers who have been born, raced, and died since the Nazarene first stepped onto the track.

What I am inviting you to do in this cool down part of our shared race is employ what I have called "metaskills" thinking to learn some large lessons from this profound story. It is quite a common term on the internet now, but in the mid-'90s I proposed and trademarked this word, metaskills, to describe some of the thinking I was doing around spirituality and work. *Meta* is a word that means "above and beyond," as in *meta*physics, where it applies to things outside of normal physics. It also contains ideas of the next level up, as in *meta*data, which is data about data. So data may be a whole set of questions from a questionnaire returned by individuals, but the *meta*data is what emerges when you put them together and get an idea of trends. The same idea is found in the word *meta*narrative, in which a number of smaller stories or episodes are put together and a larger, more comprehensive story or narrative emerges. Additionally, *meta* can refer to change, as in the word *meta*morphosis, when a chrysalis changes form and becomes a butterfly.

So *meta* means above and beyond, big-picture, top-level perspective, and it also means change. Metaskills, then, have to do with big-picture, change issues, and the skill is to see them, work with them, and live them out.

When we apply metaskills thinking to the seven sentences from the cross, two things happen. First, you can see that each one of the sentences has a metaskill contained in it. Second, you can start to see them as a set or whole. And third, you can see them as agents of change.

FINDING THE METASKILL

I don't propose to go into great detail, for that would defeat the object of thinking on a grand scale, but as you stand back from each of the seven moments, you may be able to see the metaskill contained in each one. The first sentence, "Father, forgive them, for they do not know what they are doing," contains a dynamic of prayer and forgiveness. As we saw, it is not just any prayer, but a prayer of identity, worth, security, and values. Both the prayer and the forgiveness combine to form a metaskill that has an underlying theme of letting go. Through this type of prayer, you let go of your reliance on secondary factors such as intellect and status for your sense of worth and security, and learn to develop a deep sense of identity and a total, profound trust in the object of your prayer. Simultaneously, you learn to let go of your anger, frustration, and bitterness in a way that releases you and those around you from the shackles of stress.

But *meta* also contains the idea of change. This first metaskill I suggest could be described as *moving from holding on to letting go*. The key dynamics are prayer and forgiveness, but they combine to enable you to stop holding on to attitudes, thoughts, and behaviors that produce stress and let them go so you will retain a racing style that reduces stress.

The second sentence we explored, "I tell you the truth, today you will be with me in paradise," contains elements of hope and encouragement. It is all about being good news in a pressurized environment, and as you have seen, it produces whispers of paradise. The meta idea here is that of learning to become very focused on the needs of those around you, and pass to them tailor-made gifts to enable them to find their way home. This could be described as giving away. The change dynamic can be seen if I describe the metaskill as *moving from keeping back to giving away*. Instead of hiding hope and encouragement, you give it openly and freely. It is an outward-focused skill that involves thinking, listening, and understanding so you can empower others with your words, practices, and behaviors. This giving away takes place on a regular basis, but it is particularly important at crucial and vulnerable moments in the lives of people right next to you.

The third sentence, "Dear woman, here is your son... Son, here is your mother," is a powerful example of being fully in the moment and doing the right thing at the right time. We saw this was possible because Jesus was able to race with a multi-layered consciousness and respond appropriately to each circumstance. The major skill here could be described as presence – presence of heart and presence of mind matching the presence of body. The change component cannot be found by contrasting this with absence, because you will be physically present even if you are not fully present in a moment. The metaskill here could be described as *moving from confusion to presence*. In finding a sense of mission, daily focus, and moment-by-moment meaning, confusion and worry evaporate from your life, leaving a solid sense of presence and order.

The fourth sentence, "My God, my God, why have you forsaken me," is all about integrity in the face of extreme struggle. In the first skill, we identified that there are some things to let go and not hold onto. We now need to recognize that there are also some things to hold onto and not let go. While holding onto bitterness is destructive, holding onto integrity is essential. So the meta issue here is that of holding on – in the dark, when you feel alone, and when despair might be a heartbeat away. The change element, then, could be described as *moving from giving up to holding on*.

Once you enter into this kind of thinking, you may come up with alternative ways of describing the metaskill, but the important thing is that you take the opportunity to stand back and have a big-picture look so you don't get lost in the details.

Our fifth sentence was just three words, "I am thirsty," in which we found authenticity and the best expressions of human reality. The underlying dynamic of this skill can be found when you consider that things start to line up as who you are, what you understand yourself to be, and what you do are all in harmony. A word that could summarize this healthy state would be congruence. It is a coming together, a pleasant cooperation, resulting in the exhilaration of appropriate self-expression. The change dynamic is unveiled when you think of the alternative, which includes ideas of mismatch, lack of harmony, or conflict. You may like to describe the metaskill now in your own language, such as *from conflict to congruence, or from mismatch to match*. This metaskill's description will lend itself to you bringing your own taste to the words. One that appeals to me involves musical metaphors, such as from *discord to harmony*, but I particularly like the idea of *learning to sing your own song*.

The sixth lap of our shared race looked at the phrase, "It is finished," a fantastic moment of completion when years of preparation found their fulfillment. We saw that, in this moment, there was a framework of agreement providing the context for achieving results and completing tasks. Can I agree with you that you now find the metaskill for yourself in this moment? I have my ideas around fulfillment and delivery, but perhaps you could find some phrase in exploring this one from your perspective.

The final phrase, "Father, into your hands I commit my spirit," brought us back to prayer, with a slightly different emphasis, along with a solution to the puzzle of the spirit. It contains ideas of adding "Father" to all work and finally finding what you are looking for.

Again, by now, you will have your opinions, but I suggest that the metaskill could possibly be described as *moving from longing to finding*. It's important here to realize that the finding and longing are not just yours, but the Father's as well, because you will discover that his longing to find you is even greater than your longing to find him.

In this cool down part of your racing adventure, you also should consider that all of the seven sayings have something to say about each of the seven subjects. For example, although sentence one specializes in stress reduction, the other six also contribute to this, because encouragement, balance, integrity, etc., all combine to reduce unnecessary stress. Sentence five is about being real and true to yourself, in which case integrity, spirituality, and balance will help you immensely to find that authenticity you crave. This meta approach will help you see the seven sentences as a seven-part whole aimed at teaching the whole of you how to run the whole of your race.

An additional meta issue that has struck me since I first looked at these sentences this way is related to the order in which they occur, because the sentence closest to, or on each side of the one you are exploring contains helpful supporting wisdom for its neighbor. So when you think about sentence three, spoken to John and Mary about balance, on each side of it is the wisdom of encouragement and hope and being right while feeling alone. To live in the moment, you need to feed on the power of encouragement and hope, and there will be times when you have to stand alone for what is right. The learning, then, from sentences two and four provides supporting wisdom for sentence three.

The farther back you stand, the more you will be able to see a progression over the six hours. Slowly, issues resolve, from stress to struggle to completion and solutions. It is not a haphazard journey but a dignified work pattern that progresses inevitably towards completing the task in hand.

There were three prayers on that hill (one, four, and seven), three quotations (four, five, and seven), and one question (three). They were addressed to his executioners (one), a thief (two), his mother and friend (three), his God (four), some strangers (five), everybody (six), and his Father (seven). Two of them (six and seven) were cried in a loud voice, and the rest would have been spoken while gasping for air. All of human life, work, and death can be found here, and the more you look, the more you will learn lessons for your race.

After his death, two men asked the authorities for permission to give him a decent burial. Their names were Joseph and Nicodemus. They were both members of the Jewish ruling council who, just 18 hours before, had instigated proceedings to have him executed. Nicodemus had a night interview with Jesus not long before those events, when he had been advised that the best way to race involved a new start.[1] Joseph was relatively wealthy and came from a town called Aramathea.

These two were secret followers and admirers of the carpenter. They failed to stop the execution and would have been full of regret, and probably self-rebuke, at their sense of cowardice. Joseph donated his tomb and Nicodemus provided the very expensive embalming creams needed to give Jesus a dignified burial.[2] They thought they were saving his body and at least rescuing his dignity. What they didn't realize was that this body that they were saving had already rescued them, because he raced for the cowards, the brave, and all shades in-between. In other words, he raced to revolutionize the race for all rats of all eras and all times.

Now it's your turn.

---

[1] The account Nicodemus' interview can be found in John 3

[2] The account of the burial can be found in John 19:38-42

STRETCHES:
POEMS –
THE LAST SURPRISE

SEVEN LAST SENTENCES

The following poems were commissioned by Geoff Shattock and have been especially written by Godfrey Rust.[1] A consultant to the music industry, Godfrey is also one of the UK's leading Christian poets. His book, *Welcome to the Real World*, is published by Words Out (2000) and contains poems and performance pieces written over a period of twenty years.

Regarding these works, Godfrey explains his perspective:

In these seven poems, I have tried to imagine something of what might have been in Jesus' mind leading up to him speaking each of the seven phrases from the cross. It is fanciful, of course, and no one could do it justice, but God expresses himself on a human scale, and I think it is the work he gave to poets and other creative artists to try to capture a glimpse of truth and eternity in a world of mortality and illusion. There is no better subject matter for that work than man's 'execution' of God on the cross.

---

[1]   All poems are under copyright, © Godfrey Rust, 2003. These works were commissioned by Geoff Shattock for the WORKTALK Learning Program. They may be freely performed or reproduced for non-commercial purposes only. For more information about Godfrey Rust, visit www.worktalk.gs or contact him at godfrey@worktalk.gs.

ONE: FATHER FORGIVE THEM

Father forgive them for they did not know what they were looking for
when I slipped past into humanity in my now famous disguise.

My light shone strangely in the dark of a desire they could not
comprehend.
Forgive them for they did not know what I was doing.

The streets were full of people saying *Peace Peace*, but there is no peace
for I came to bring a sword that would be used against me.
Forgive them for they could not know the price of an immortal's
suicide.

They tried with all they had to keep us from this meeting here.
Father forgive them for they do not know what we are doing.

They were so negligent I almost got away.
How hard it was to be the silent Word.
At the last I had to spell it out —
You have said it: I am a king.
What you must do, do quickly.

Forgive them all, my dear beloved dull accomplices
following orders from another kingdom.
Forgive the crowds who made the right choice of Barabbas.
Forgive Pilate's wife, whose conscience almost ruined everything.

Forgive them for they do not know what they were building.
I was the architect and these rough beams
were cut to meet my most exacting standards.

Forgive them for they do not know what will be executed here.
How could they understand these hammer blows

would be the final acts of our creation?

Like workmen at the launch of some great enterprise of state
they gather faithfully to watch the ceremony of our fierce ambition,
and as they hoist me up to you
before this brutal act of love obliterates my mortal life completely,
Father forgive them for they do not know what they are doing.

TWO: I TELL YOU THE TRUTH

All those deceptions:
nothing is what it seemed.
Hopeless. No way back
and no way down.
Nowhere to turn
but over in your mind
and it's all over.
No mistake but yours.
No more chances, just
this last surprise, a God
dying next to you. It took
a lot to nail you down
and gain your attention. Strange
to find that after all
you were the victim. Stranger still
that robbed of hope your prayer
is answered, and you will see
one last deception unmasked here.
Nothing is what it seems.
This desolate place
is entrance to my kingdom, and
I tell you the truth, today
you will be with me in paradise.

THREE: WOMAN

Woman, as I prepare
to slip the leash of time

for a moment your grief
reels me back in; the sword

pierces us both
but you alone will feel then

the pain I feel now,
watching a mother

watch a son die. Before
you gave birth to me

I AM, and at a word
I set time flowing

like tears: but what
could I in my eternity

know of such loss as yours? Timeless
I became mankind —

there was no other way
to learn the meaning

of this moment. Soon
I will have gained

eternity again; you have
the meantime, and I will

not leave you comfortless.
Beside you is one

whom I have loved
more than a brother:

Dear woman, here is your son.
Son, here is your mother.

FOUR: TO BE HUMAN

To be human is to deal with death,
and I have wagered all to taste the fruit

of this desperate new Eden. To be human
is to court the risk of failure, and so I

embrace this tree of knowledge of despair.
And to be human is to know that God

may be illusion, and so I have made myself
human enough for doubt and disbelief.

What else is left for God to understand?
Faith is the gamble of a dying man.

The condemned son crying out into the dark
guesses his father hears, yet does not come.

What kind of love is this that keeps such silence?
My God, my God, why have you forsaken me?

FIVE: I THIRST

Nothing
up my sleeve.
There's no sleeve.

Look on
your naked God.
Look on
your reflection.

Follow me
and show
humanity
like this.

This is
the tree
of life.

You need me.
I chose
to need you —

to love you
God became
animal.

Help me.
I thirst.

SIX: I SAW IT FIRST

I saw it first, this bloody work of heart,
conceived in my mind's eye *in the beginning*,

or what you call the beginning. Time
was the canvas I prepared to paint on.

I drew its outline in the life of Abraham,
my palette history, its colors mixed

in Israel's rise and fall. I worked from life:
against a landscape of an Eden spoiled

my people with their untamed rebel hearts
stared out through masks of beauty scarred with sin.

Painstaking detail. Light and darkness. Then
the hardest thing I ever did. Love

was daubed with every brush-stroke of the Spirit
on the ungiving texture of the soul.

Finally to shape the central figure
I needed human hands. I labored with Mary

to bring the enterprise to birth. Three more decades
of preparation were meticulous —

it is not irony that I was framed
and hung up here to die: it is the point.

I am the artist and the portrait too,
painting out at last in the blood of God

a perfect self-expression: my still life.
This is my masterpiece and *it is finished*.

SEVEN: I HAVE TRAVELED

I have traveled light, so that the leaving
should be easier. What I bequeath

is left according to your will
and this new testament: I leave a church

to be built on a broken rock. I leave
nothing written down: I heard my words

blown freely on the winds of Galilee
to seed the fertile hearts of men. I leave

no money, debts or property, no house
for shrine, no artifact for relic. I leave just

the remnants of a meal. My cloak
is cast aside and gambled for. I leave

no tomb to raid, no corpse to disinter,
no fingerprints, no blood, no DNA.

I could have gained the world, but now
nothing stands between us except this

last legacy. Because it is written; because
it is the only pledge by which all souls

that fill the devil's pawnshop are redeemed;
and because until I give it up to you

it cannot be returned to anyone,
Father, into your hands I commit my spirit.

THE LAST SURPRISE
BY GEOFF SHATTOCK

In the end, the seven sentences we have studied are words of love designed to woo a wayward world and, as such, can be seen as a sonnet or love poem from the heart of the Divine to any and all who would learn to run the race in His profound company. Here is a way of seeing the sonnet:

THE LAST SURPRISE

Father...
Forgive them
For
They don't know
What they do
You'll be
With Me
In paradise
I'm telling
You
The truth

Son...
Here is
Your mother
Dear woman
Here's your son
My God
My God
Why
Have you
Forsaken
Forsaken

Me?...
I'm thirsty
It is finished
My spirit
I commit
Into
Your hands
Father
I commit
My

Spirit…

– *Geoff Shattock*

ABOUT THE AUTHOR:
THE RACE SO FAR

Geoff Shattock was born just over a hundred miles north of London, and has lived in London most of his life. From an early age, five key themes characterized his life – a love of music, science, sport, spirituality, and humor.

His love of music took him into the school choir as lead soloist and later into guitar and vocals as he teamed up with poet Godfrey Rust. With Geoff as the band's main singer/songwriter, they have released three albums and occasionally reunite to unleash their eclectic musical forms on unsuspecting audiences.

Shattock's scientific journey led him to a high-school major biology prize before taking his first degree in physiology at London University. And 20 years later, it led to his master's in the psychobiology of stress, when he completed a research thesis on the impact of faith on occupational stress.

His sporting exploits have included soccer, basketball (until everyone else grew), track, squash, and the incomparable sport of champions, ping pong – yes, the *sport*, not the "game" – while his most marked achievements came in the field of injuries. However, unable to admit aging, he continues to run (including half marathons) and persists in the illusion that, one day, he will beat his son-in-law at ping pong and reclaim the champion's title. Additionally, Geoff was introduced all-too-late to American football and is now a distant fan and arm-chair coach of the Jacksonville Jaguars.

Geoff's spiritual journey combined with all of his passions as he developed an integrated approach to science and theology while studying for his Cambridge University diploma in religious studies at the London School of Theology. That combination resulted in him regularly serving as a sports director for Christian youth camps and building his musical repertoire with an emphasis on spiritual meanings.

After working as a national and local pastor, director of an inner-city Christian center, and advisor for 280 London Baptist churches, Geoff founded WORKTALK in 1997 with friend and now-Chairman, Simon Constantine. Over the years, this spiritual journey has explored life skills, psychospirituality, anger management, life balance, and personal development, and has involved coaching, training, and consulting.

Geoff describes his purpose in life as "to find angles so that people can see Jesus of Nazareth in a way they have not seen him before." Over the years, through preaching, teaching, training, writing, music, sports, and humor, Geoff has tried to find these angles. In so doing, he has helped remove unnecessary pain from people's lives, and *Jesus and the Racing Rat* is a culminating expression of all these themes.

Since 1997, Geoff has become one of the leading thinkers in the spirituality-and-work movement, and has worked with churches, charities, businesses, and individuals to help them find better ways to work based on healthy spiritual, integrated, and practical foundations.

Geoff is married to Maria, who is from Lisbon, Portugal – they met while studying at the London School Of Theology in 1977. Maria is a senior media resources officer in an inner-city school and has a remarkable journey of her own. She specializes in capturing the ideas that others wish to communicate, and she transforms these ideas into visual expressions for them in order to celebrate the learning process. Geoff and Maria have one married daughter, Suzy, who is a medical professional and developing a journey of her own.

RELATED RESOURCES:
FROM WORKTALK

DVD SERIES

Geoff Shattock has recorded a DVD series also based on the seven last sentences from the carpenter's cross. Entitled WORKTALK, it is designed for individuals and small or large groups to use as a learning course. Each powerful talk takes you into the work-related areas covered in this book and provides you with a great toolkit for group discussion. The DVD series comes with a comprehensive handbook and on-screen tips and advice from Geoff Shattock to enable you to get the maximum benefit from the curriculum. The WORKTALK DVD series can be ordered from www.worktalk.gs/shop.

DVD Series Pack US Edition (includes one handbook)
– ISBN 978-0-9553560-9-4
Additional Handbook US Edition
– ISBN 978-0-9553560-8-7
DVD Series Pack UK Edition (includes one handbook)
– ISBN 978-0-9553650-0-1
Additional Handbook UK Edition
– ISBN 978-1-9029771-1-9

FREE E-MAIL WEEKLY

Each week, Geoff Shattock writes a thought-provoking, spiritually based, work-related e-mail called "WORKTALKweekly." If you want weekly help with your personal race, sign up for free support at www.worktalk.gs/solutions/weekly.

GEOFF SHATTOCK IN PERSON

If you would like Geoff Shattock to speak at your event, seminar, conference, or church, please send an e-mail to comms@worktalk.gs and we will make arrangements with you. We can also design individualized training for you and your staff.

JESUS AND THE RACING RAT SPECIAL EDITIONS

If you would like to have a special, customized edition of *Jesus and the Racing Rat* produced with your logo on the back cover for you to sell to your members at a special rate, e-mail comms@worktalk.gs for details.

Details of all WORKTALK resources can be found at
www.worktalk.gs.
To purchase additional copies of this book, visit
www.worktalk.gs/shop.

Visit the official *Jesus and the Racing Rat* web site at www.racingrat.gs.

CONTACT INFORMATION

WORKTALK USA
PO Box 351257
Jacksonville, FL
32235-1257

WORKTALK UK
56 Baldry Gardens
London SW16 3DJ
Tel. +44 20 8764 8080

comms@worktalk.gs
www.worktalk.gs

SPACE FOR YOUR RACE: FOR YOUR NOTES, REFLECTIONS, JOURNALING – OR A TO-DO LIST

NOTES

NOTES